OWL
LIGHT

OWL
LIGHT

The Unique Story of a Boy and his Owl

JON HADWICK

KYLE CATHIE LIMITED

First published 1991 in Great Britain by
Kyle Cathie Limited
3 Vincent Square, London SW1P 2LX

ISBN 1 85626 027 5

Jon Hadwick is hereby identified as author of this
work in accordance with Section 77 of the Copyright,
Designs and Patents Act 1988.

A CIP catalogue record for this book is available from the
British Library

Designed by Behram Kapadia
Typeset by DP Photosetting, Aylesbury, Bucks
Printed by Butler and Tanner Ltd, Frome, Somerset

I would like to dedicate this book to my family and all my relatives: my mother, Sandra, my sisters, Leanne and Anna-Marie, and my father, Paul, now separated. I would especially like to thank my grandmother, Jean, and my uncle, Barry, for their generosity and kindness in helping me with financial backing and support with my artwork.

Acknowledgements

I would like to thank Frank Almond for his painstaking help with the writing of this book, and also to thank Derek and Val for allowing me to keep owls at their place and Maureen and Aubrey Edwards for their enormous generosity and kindness in helping me to learn about birds, their habits and medical care.

Contents

Introduction

I first became interested in birds of prey when I was about five, and my parents used to take me to the local zoo in Colchester, Essex. They had quite a few birds of prey there – owls, falcons, even the odd eagle – and after a few visits I was making a beeline for the huge cages that housed these magnificent creatures. By the time I was twelve I felt ready to acquire my own bird of prey, and although Barny turned out to be a disaster, I gained a lot of experience – even if much of it was painful.

Perhaps the most important thing was that Barny was a barn owl. I never set out to have a barn owl – they're notoriously difficult to train, I was told, and are no use for most aspects of falconry – but Barny was the only bird around at the time that I could afford. And if I hadn't had Barny, I might not have bought my second barn owl, Dawn, who is so special to me, and who you'll be reading a lot about in this book. So Barny did set me on the road to training, breeding and eventually releasing barn owls back into the wild.

It's hard, thinking back to those days, to put my finger on exactly what got me hooked on these birds. I just seem always to have been interested in wildlife, and birds in particular. Although no one in my family was passionate about animals, it was obviously in *my* blood. My Uncle Barry always encouraged me and was forever telling people that one day I would be an ornithologist or a conservationist. I, on the other hand, didn't dare to think that I could turn my dream into a reality.

Until recently, I couldn't imagine it would be possible for me to spend all my time working with birds, but the way things have gone over the last few years I can scarcely see myself doing anything else. I'm lucky to have had the encouragement I have had from my family – especially my uncle and my nan. If ever I have doubts about what I'm trying to do, my uncle keeps telling me I'm right, and that's so important to me.

I was on holiday in Grimsby recently – that's well over three hundred miles from my home in North Cornwall – when a man pointed at me in the street and said, 'Hey, you're that boy with the owl!' The local press had done an article on me because British Telecom had used Dawn in an advertising promotion, and the man had recognised me from my picture in the newspaper. I felt famous. I'd already had quite a bit of publicity in my own local papers; then the nationals picked up on my story, and Dawn and I had our pictures in the *Daily Telegraph* and the *Independent*. Seeing our pictures and names in print seemed very odd and unreal at the time. It was as if they were writing about someone else, but at the same time, I knew what I was reading was true – it really was us!

Dawn took it much more coolly. When I showed her our picture, she just blinked as if to say, 'Well, yes, of course – so what?' But Mum bought up half the paper shop, dozens of copies at a time of anything we were in, so she could show friends and send cuttings to relatives. It was flattering and embarrassing at the same time.

I'm a bit more used to the publicity now, and I realise that it can be a good thing, for two reasons. First, keeping birds of prey is an expensive business, and if I'm to go on doing it, the bits of sponsorship I've had will be very useful. But second, and more importantly, it shows that lots of people must really care about what I'm doing. Newspapers wouldn't write about me and TV crews wouldn't film me and Dawn if they didn't think their audiences would be interested. And that's great, because the only thing that will save barn owls – and any other endangered species – from extinction is people knowing and caring about the problems they face.

By the time this book comes out, I'll still only be seventeen, but I already feel I've achieved quite a lot. Those early days at Colchester Zoo are still fresh in my mind, and my passion for the birds hasn't lessened a bit. What I've added to it is a bit more knowledge of what makes birds of prey tick, and a lot more determination to work with them and for them for the rest of my life. They'll always be my first love, and if in the course of this book I can make you share some of my enthusiasm, that'll be one more ambition fulfilled.

1

The Young Ornithologist

I still don't really know what it was about birds of prey that fascinated me. Somehow, even at the age of five when I made my first visits to Colchester Zoo, I felt they stood out from other birds. It must have been their sheer size and the impression of power you got even when they were standing still. A squawking, dayglo-coloured parrot was no match for, say, the majestic eagle owl with its camouflage plumage, massive wings and awesome beak and talons. I was also taken by the way the cute-looking tawny owls just sat there on their perches, looking at each other with one eye open. I know now that owls are not at all like living cuddly toys, but at the time I wanted to reach out and cuddle them.

Even more than their magnificent appearance, I think it was the movement of the birds that captivated me – their ability to fly fast or, in the case of the owls, slow and in absolute silence, and pinpoint their prey with breathtaking accuracy, even in total darkness. There were lanner falcons and peregrines in the zoo, I remember, and I still find their perfect manoeuvrability in the air almost unbeliev-able. Simply by shuffling their tail feathers like a pack of cards, they can hang in the air or spin round at breakneck speed.

Years later, at a falconry centre, I once saw a falcon miss the bait it was supposed to pick up, fly past, come to a sudden standstill in mid-air, turn 180 degrees and zoom down again. No fighter aircraft could do it.

After all these years of watching birds of prey in flight, I still find that they will do something completely unexpected. You just don't get the same sort of thrill from watching blackbirds.

The life of a five-year-old ornithologist did not always run smoothly. One day I found a dead blackbird, already in an advanced state of decay, in the road outside my house. Reverently I picked it up and buried it in our back garden – three feet down seemed to me an appropriate depth. A few days later, a lady who lived across the road made the mistake of asking me what sort of bird it had been. I promptly dug the poor bird up and presented it to her. She was not

Osprey

amused. I was always giving secret funerals to dead birds. There must have been dozens of them in our back garden by the time I was seven, though my parents had no idea they were living next to a bird cemetery. Even the compost heap had corpses in it.

We used to live about a hundred yards away from the main park in Colchester. The park had a few fairly large hills (or so it seemed to me at the time) topped by a castle, a lake with a river running through it and quite a few trees scattered here and there. It wasn't exactly a naturalist's dream, but to me it was the Great Outdoors, an unexplored wilderness. Walking along the riverbank or lakeside, I could see a variety of waterfowl, such as moorhens, seagulls and ducks; up in the trees were virtually the entire crow family – jays, rooks and jackdaws – as well as blackbirds, thrushes, finches, all the everyday birds. And up on the hill, the castle was home to the pigeons, who would retire there to roost after a busy day's scavenging in the town centre. Whenever my mother had to go shopping I'd contrive to make her walk to the high street via the park. All the way I'd be talking to myself in my head, saying, 'Um, yes, that's a so-and-so,' practising my identification skills. My grand-mother is a keen birdwatcher and she'd already introduced me to a lot of the different birds that visited her bird-table, telling me what they ate and showing me their nests and explaining how they were made and what they were made of.

As I got older, about seven or eight, I was allowed to go to the park on my own. Now, instead of simply cataloguing the different species in my head, I could start to explore their habitat and study their behaviour. I was in my element.

There was a sort of bird sanctuary on an island in the middle of the lake and I'd spend a lot of my time watching the comings and goings of the inhabitants. I just never got bored. But fascinated as I was by these aquatic birds, I longed to see the falcons and owls I'd seen at the zoo flying free, and this is a rare occurrence. In fact, the only bird of prey I ever saw hovering over the park was a kestrel.

When I did spot the kestrel, I would sit down on the ground or the nearest bench and gaze in amazement. At this time I was at a loss to understand how it managed to hover for so long in the same place. I would sit there for ages trying to figure out how it accomplished this. I didn't know anything about the way some birds use warm air currents to help their flight. One theory I came up with was that the

Owl Light

BELOW Dawn and me in St Nectan's Glen. A path through a mile of woodland leads to the waterfall. It's a beautiful place for any nature lover, and I did a lot of my early birdwatching in Cornwall here.

RIGHT A clump of woodland on a farm near where I live. Tawny owls live here – the trees form a corridor across the farm where they can hunt without venturing out on to open land. The overgrown grass, hedges and piles of wood are a haven for mice, which are among the tawnies' favourite food.

ABOVE LEFT This is a tawny owl that was found injured by the side of the road and brought to my neighbour, Maureen Edwards, for help. We called her Rusty, because of her colour. She's very easy to handle and not fierce at all, so she had obviously been hand-reared. She might have been released by someone who doesn't like seeing birds in cages, or by the breeder – perhaps he didn't have a licence to keep her and somebody reported him. Anyway, she's far too tame to survive in the wild, so she lives quite happily at Maureen's.

LEFT Rusty and another tawny owl, Herbert. As you can see, he's much greyer than she is, which is rare – both sexes of tawnies are usually the same colour. Herbert came from a breeder who had gone on holiday without realising his owl had laid eggs. By the time he came back, Herbert was too big to be ringed, so it would have been illegal to sell him. He came to live at Maureen's, too, and she may well breed him with Rusty – if we're right in thinking Rusty is a female, that is!

ABOVE As time went by, more and more people started bringing me injured birds to look after. This barn owl's broken wing had been set by a vet who kept it in a cat cage for a week or two so that it could rest. The bird has become very unfit, and the damaged wing is shorter than the other, so I've been working on moving it in the way the bird would move it in flight, to stretch it. At the moment, it doesn't seem to be working and it may be that we can never return this owl to the wild – it certainly wouldn't survive as it is. But it will still be useful for breeding.

21

LEFT Ruffling up the feathers to make yourself look bigger is a common defensive measure in a lot of birds. That's what this juvenile male barn owl is doing; Barny turned out to have more violent tendencies than this! (Jane Burton/Bruce Coleman Ltd)

BELOW LEFT A pair of barn owls with young. The chicks are only a few days old, but these parents are obviously more relaxed with them than the Barnys were with any of their offspring. (Kim Taylor/Bruce Coleman Ltd)

BELOW These chicks hatched two days apart – when this picture was taken they were 29, 27 and 25 days old, but you can see the heart-shaped facial disc emerging clearly from the ball of fluff. Dawn was younger than this when I first had her. (Jane Burton/Bruce Coleman Ltd)

It's difficult to imagine a newborn chick turning into a beautiful bird like the barn owl. This one is about three hours old and still lying in the foetal position in which it emerged from the egg.
(Jane Burton/Bruce Coleman Ltd)

down beat of its wings pushed it upwards and the up beat pushed it downwards and the two cancelled each other out so that the kestrel stayed where it was. Completely inaccurate, of course, but not bad for a seven-year-old.

As I sat looking up at this magnificent bird, especially on a fine day, I used to feel a terrific urge to see a bird of prey flying to a lure, which I'd read about in my falconry books. I think my desire to train a bird of my own must have been born right there in Colchester Park. I used to wonder just what the kestrel was looking at, what it was thinking, and I'd imagine how wonderful it must be to be suspended in mid-air, looking down on the Earth as it was.

Given the chance, I would have stayed watching or followed the kestrel around the park all day, but if I was on a shopping sortie with my mother, she was always in an incredible hurry, so that wasn't possible. When I did manage to follow it, I was stunned by the fact that it could gain such a good speed although it was flying without putting any apparent effort into beating its wings. Then it would presumably spot some potential prey and come to a standstill in mid-air as if it had brakes.

One thing I distinctly remember about watching that kestrel hover happened on a clear blue day when I'd managed to position myself practically underneath the bird. I noticed that its wing and tail feathers faded out gradually as they got further away from its body, so that the sun was peering through near the tips as the feathers became thinner. I always used to relate this to the ghostly effect you sometimes get round a figure in a horror film.

Watching the kestrel was a great experience, but life was still very frustrating for me because my mother understandably wouldn't let me wander very far afield, and I wasn't going to see my first real live wild owl in Colchester Park! Tantalisingly, at night, I might hear the plaintive hoot of a tawny owl somewhere in the trees, beyond my little world. I was already enough of an expert to recognise it – people had begun to give me books about birds of prey, so the first time I heard this sorrowful sound I searched through my books until I found out what it was. In fact, tawnies are the only British owls that hoot – some of them screech, but little owls whistle and barn owls make a terrible snorting sound like an old man snoring. They can also produce a loud hissing, screeching noise.

I kept reading and my knowledge kept growing, but I still wanted to see an owl's nest and experience the thrill of actually seeing one in flight, in the feather, so to speak. The birds in the aviary at the zoo were enchanting, but I wanted more. Besides, my frequent visits there were becoming expensive.

It was around this time that I first discovered the darker side of ornithology – the effect of man on the environment. I know now that every park, meadow, lake, river, moor and garden in Britain is in need of conservation, as much as any game reserve in Africa or rain forest in South America. But it was in Colchester Park that I had my first lesson in conservation in microcosm, if you like.

The problem with the lake in the park was that local fishermen wanted to fish in it. And when they fished there they would inevitably lose tackle, and it would stay in the lake forming a hazard for the ducks and swans. On a number of occasions I saw birds entangled in these 'snares'. I'd often see birds with gut or wire wrapped around their necks or wings, or looking ill because, as I discovered later, they'd swallowed lead shot which the anglers used to weight their lines. There were even birds with hooks embedded in their webbed feet.

Although I knew it wasn't my fault, I always felt frustrated because I couldn't do anything to help. I also felt strangely guilty, almost ashamed. I was so close to these birds, they were like friends, and it seemed I had a personal responsibility towards them. Obviously this sense of guilt, this idea that I had betrayed a friendship, spurred me on when I got older, not only to study birds but also actively to promote their well-being and do what I could to prevent their numbers from dwindling. But at the time I was just hurt that I couldn't wade out into the lake and save them. Of course I was far too small, and they'd have swum away from me in fright anyway, but that didn't stop me trying on occasion.

I can still recall one particularly sad instance. When I went over to the lake one day I spotted a seagull in distress. It was just floating on the surface, not wading or swimming, but unnaturally afloat; so exhausted it couldn't even sit upright. Its head bowed, its wings half open and useless, it was very, very wearily steering itself round and round in hopeless circles. I could tell it was virtually on the point of death. My heart cried out to it, but when I approached it, it summoned up the last dregs of its strength and paddled frantically away to the middle of the lake, where I had been instructed never to go. Even from the shore I could tell that it had half strangled itself in a length of fishing line; it was also hooked up in several places and carrying some heavy land weights. Soon I, too, was very distressed, but I knew that it was going to be dead within a few hours, and I was helpless. I didn't know about the RSPB or the RSPCA or any other caring agency I could have turned to for assistance. At my tender age, I could only look on.

The next morning I was back in the park. I walked around the lake three times, looking for the gull. On the third circuit, I found it, lying dead in a reed bed. I had a fishing net with me and carefully fished it out. When I had a close look at it, I saw that the inside of its mouth, which should have been pink, was very pale and frothing. The body was still warm. I imagined its tragic, night-long struggle to survive, the suffering it had endured and its final painful death as the sun rose. I felt very angry.

As I untangled the fishing tackle, I found over three feet of wire line, two hooks and five weights. It was obvious what had happened. The whole lake was a death trap for birds. And I knew why. Every time an angler casts and curses when he loses his line, I, too, now curse as I think of some wild creature getting enmeshed in the deadly snare he has inadvertently set. Fishing is the most popular outdoor sport in the British Isles, so just think how many weights and hooks and miles of wire and gut are accidentally lost each year off our coasts and in our lakes and rivers. And imagine what the death toll of wildlife must be.

Fortunately, fishing is banned in the lake in Colchester Park now, and restricted to a few responsible permit-holders along the river. These are, at least, moves in the right direction.

The ducks that lived on the island in that lake didn't restrict their activities to the park. Mallards, coots and moorhens could often be seen and heard waddling about the housing estate where I lived or sometimes even boldly marching up the high street. There were platoons of them on a sort of scrounging patrol, begging food from gardeners or shoppers. Often these sorties would result in a skirmish with the pigeons, who presumably saw the ducks as invaders on their patch. Greatly outnumbered, the ducks would abandon their foraging mission and beat a hasty retreat to their island stronghold at the slightest sign of trouble. But we always encouraged them at our house by putting out tempting bowlfuls of soggy bread and milk.

After a while the ducks got so confident that they'd come right into our garden and eventually into the house itself. It's funny to look back and think how much my mum enjoyed having the ducks around – she encouraged them as much as I did. But later she developed an allergy to feathers, and that made it very difficult for her when I wanted to keep birds in the house!

We'd been feeding 'our' ducks for about three months when one day, much to my disappointment, they mysteriously disappeared. We kept putting food out, though, and after about a month they all suddenly returned, with hordes of hungry ducklings in tow. The new mothers were ravenous and it was easy to coax them back into the house. I decided to try an experiment. I wanted to see if our guests could be persuaded to climb the stairs, so I laid a trail of bread from the bowl in the hall up to my bedroom. And I waited.

I had a long wait. Webbed feet were not designed for mountaineering, but after a few weeks the ducks had devised a method of hopping up the stairs one at a time, eating every morsel of bread along the way, until finally they were actually in my bedroom. I was thrilled. It was the first time I had ever trained a bird to do something I wanted it to do. They would never stay in my bedroom very long, but you can imagine my excitement each lunchtime as I watched them arrive in the garden, enter the house and quack their way up to me, as regular as clockwork.

I must have been about six or seven at this time. Little did I know then that one day I would be training a fully grown bird of prey to hunt.

From my bedroom I had quite a clear view of the lake between two neighbouring houses. I didn't own a pair of binoculars, so I couldn't observe the birds as closely as I'd have wished, but I had something much closer to watch. In summer the estate became the home of colonies of house martins and swallows. Every house seemed to have at least one, sometimes several, of the distinctive mud-baked nests under its eaves. We used to have a family of martins nesting directly over our front porch, just under my bedroom window. They'd come back every year and I learned a lot about their breeding habits, watching both parents bring food back to the chicks. I was intrigued to find that they might have two or even three broods in a summer, and that the elder chicks sometimes stayed around in the nest after the younger ones had hatched.

Obviously I enjoyed having the opportunity to watch any nesting birds so close at hand – I could reach out of my bedroom window, when Mum wasn't around, and feel right inside the nest – but many of the neighbours looked on the house martins as pests who infested their property and made a mess. Even my father wasn't too pleased about continually having to clean his porch roof, which our residents had covered in droppings and other nest debris. Eventually he decided to give them their marching orders, and one spring, just before the birds were due to arrive, he nailed wire netting and a large dustbin bag along the eaves to stop them building their nests in the usual place. This did the trick, of course, but the birds simply moved in next door, which didn't make the neighbours too happy.

I was sad to see the martins go, even though they had often been very noisy at night and kept me awake. Perhaps they are pests to a lot of people, but we didn't see too many flies around our estate during the hot summer, so they had their uses.

By this time I was a serious amateur naturalist with a special interest in anything in feathers. I didn't completely exclude other creatures, though. My second favourite place at the zoo was the Reptile House, and I've had various sorts of reptiles as pets. Now I use their old vivarium to rear owls in. But birds were my great passion. I studied nests, eggs, flight, breeding habits, feeding habits, anything and everything to do with birds.

I had also begun to keep a notebook in which I wrote details of my observations, complete with explanatory drawings. I'd been drawing since I was tiny – my grandfather is a very good artist, although he specialises in landscapes, and he'd helped me enormously from the beginning. I used to sit and watch him for hours, painstakingly working on a painting, and, following his example, I would push myself harder and harder to make my own drawings better. The drawing and the birdwatching had grown up as complementary interests from a very young age. I find it hard to believe that my paintings now sell in London and many other places!

Not long after I'd started the notebook, I became the proud owner of my first pair of binoculars. I'd spotted them in a second-hand shop and immediately began saving feverishly to make them mine before anyone else got their hands on them. At last I had five pounds – but when my father and I went to buy them we were told that they cost fifteen pounds, a considerable sum of money to an eight-year-old, and way beyond my means. Good old Dad, however, did the decent thing and the binoculars were mine. They were excellent binoculars, too, and I had hours and hours of pleasure with them. I've still got them, in fact.

There was no stopping me now. I was a fully equipped birdwatcher, very inexperienced, perhaps, but with a one-track mind. My birdwatching vigils lasted for hours: spying on swallows and swifts as they flitted over the lake, scooping up water or snapping up insects. When I wasn't in the park, I was cataloguing the host of visitors to the weeping willow tree on our front lawn – just about everything that would sit in a tree came there, mostly blackbirds, sparrows and pigeons, but the ducks loved the shelter of the drooping branches. I became a total bird addict.

But there was still no sign of the elusive owl, and now I had another quest, too. One particular bird was driving me crazy. I knew what it looked like, I knew what it sounded like, I had read all about it. Its ringing, double-noted call haunted me night after night – a call the least experienced birdwatcher would recognise instantly. But I just couldn't spot one. The bird in question was the common cuckoo.

I was learning the most important attribute of any budding ornithologist – patience. It was to be seven long years before I actually clapped eyes on a cuckoo in the wild – on a school camping holiday to the Scilly Isles, of all places – but that was in another life and another land, far from my roots in Colchester Park and Colchester Zoo. Because in 1982, when I was nine years old, my father's work brought us to North Cornwall, where the landscapes are among the most magical on Earth and the legend of King Arthur still burns.

2

Cornwall

At first Cornwall was a bit strange to me. We'd made three or four visits to the area to look around before we finally moved down, but I had no real idea what was happening. It was all just a big adventure. Then one day I found myself sitting in a packed car and we were away and moving into a new house in a place called Tintagel. It was during the Easter holidays and the streets were full of holiday-makers – I would be seeing a lot of them in the future. One thing that I had grasped about the whole business was that we were going to live in a country area where there would be lots of wildlife, and I had heard of King Arthur, of course.

What with all the activity associated with moving house, it was two weeks before we got to see Arthur's famous castle. I'd been expecting a great hall with a giant round table, towering turrets, a moat and a drawbridge, but, of course, it turned out to be a ruin. Still, it's a magnificent place, perched on a great rock jutting out into the sea and with commanding views. It was easy to imagine that it might have been Camelot, like in the picture story-books I'd read. But really it was the buzzards and the kestrels circling overhead that caught my eye as we made our way down the coastal path.

I'd see both these birds in the zoo, so I was fascinated to see them in the wild. By now I'd read about how exhausting flight could be and how birds of prey used warm air currents – known as thermals – to lift them without using up too much energy, and here they were, doing just that over the rocks by Tintagel Castle. They were looking for food, of course, and would suddenly plunge downwards at lightning speed when they spotted something. A kestrel's prey might be something as small as a beetle, and as they tend to hover twenty or thirty feet above the ground, their eyesight and the accuracy of their dive are both awe-inspiring.

The day after we first visited the castle, my sister and I were treated to a walk along the cliffs. North Cornwall must have some of the most spectacular scenery in the whole of the British Isles, and the coastline from Morwenstow to Looe consists of wild, towering cliffs that are so rugged many people have lost their lives on them. On a wet winter's day when the sea is at its roughest, the sight of the waves pounding against the bottom of the cliffs, throwing spray up over the top and into the fields, is breathtaking. In the summer, on the other hand, the sea is a beautiful dark blue and the sunlight glistens like tinsel on the surface of the water. Then the cliffs come alive with sea birds gliding effortlessly along the coastline on fishing or scavenging expeditions. They range from the common but splendid gulls to the truly magnificent gannets; shags and cormorants, which look very much alike and are fabulous divers; razorbills, which in my view look more like penguins; guillemots and of course the famous puffin, which lives mainly on some of the many rugged islands just off shore.

Another feature of the coast is the number of inlets like the one at Rock, near Padstow. Some of these inlets lead to salt marshes and estuaries which give refuge to many other coastal birds, especially waders. The muddy or sandy beds and long damp grass make ideal habitat for such birds as dunlin, which are mainly seen in winter, and of course a variety of ducks and geese. There are mallards, teals, of which I have seen a few recently in the Camel estuary, always an abundance of moorhens and coots, and here and there the odd tern. I have never seen an avocet in Cornwall, but I'm told that this rare and unique bird has been spotted on these marshes.

The water itself also has a wealth of life. You will often find starfish in pools on the beach, and there are always plenty of gobies and blennies. The seas are full of mackerel, pollock, dogfish, wrass, conger eels and a variety of flat fish, just to name a few, so the fishing is great.

Going inland, you first come across the Cornish farmland. You notice immediately that it is different from other parts of the country, because the roads are very narrow and windy and the hedges well built and in most cases so tall they are impossible to see over. In the summer these hedges come alive with colour and activity. There's an amazing variety of wild flowers, insects, birds and other wildlife.

Rabbits and foxes are common enough to be regarded as a nuisance; there are also hedgehogs, voles, mice and other rodents. Most of the animals that live along the hedgerows unfortunately only come out at night and the best way to see them is in the light of a car's headlamp. My favourite of these creatures is the badger. I spend many evenings with a spotlight just roaming the fields and observing what they and the other animals are doing, and I thoroughly enjoy myself.

Because of the rabbits and rodents, some of which do of course appear during the day, there are also large numbers of birds of prey. The most frequently seen in Cornwall is the common buzzard, which flourishes because of the huge rabbit population. Its equivalent among the nocturnal birds is the tawny owl. Although there are not all that many trees in North Cornwall, those that are there, are usually found in large groups, which the tawny owl loves. There are also kestrels, the occasional harrier, and various owls: barn owls are decreasing in number, but if you're lucky you'll also see little owls, short- and long-eared owls – they're all found in or near woodland.

Further inland, you find yourself climbing on to the moors, which are another haven for wildlife. Bleak and lonely they may be, but they are covered with lakes and pools which house frogs, toads, newts, eels and freshwater fish, while on the banks you'll find vermin such as water rats, stoats, weasels and the like. These do occur on the farmland, too, but not in such numbers and they're much more difficult to see there. You can sometimes spot deer on the moors, though they also occur nearer the coast, mainly in the woodland areas but occasionally in the open fields too.

Like the coast, the moors are very rugged in places. High peaks are crested with boulders worn smooth by the weather. There's a great variety of bracken, ferns and other plant life. But the real attractions are the fresh air and the breathtaking views. In some places on exceptionally clear days you can almost see from the south to the north coast.

For a week or so after we moved to Cornwall, I was free to have a great time exploring my new habitat. But then the dreaded word 'school' was mentioned, and I found myself decked out in a strange blue and grey uniform with a new yellow and blue tie and a starched white shirt collar that felt tight and very uncomfortable round my neck. The carefree days of the Easter holidays were over. Any kid will tell you that the worst part of moving house is having to start at a new school where you don't know anyone, and I was scared stiff.

I soon discovered that a lot of the local children stuck together and that outsiders weren't made very welcome – even if you come from another part of Cornwall it takes a long time to be accepted. The teachers were very helpful and caring, and for the first few days I thought I was getting on quite well with my new classmates. But I quickly found out that they were just 'sussing me out' – seeing how tough I was – and when my novelty as a new boy wore off, I was out in the cold. This took the form of teasing, mostly, and one day I was so fed up that I just walked out of school. A teacher came after me but I climbed through a hedge and sat tight for an hour or so.

I suppose the problem was that my interest in birds had made me a bit of a loner. I'd spent so much time on my own, sitting watching birds, or reading about them or drawing them, that I didn't make many friends, and those I had took second place to the birds. The result was that I was painfully shy. The kids at my new school all went round in little gangs, spoiling for a fight – nothing serious, just pushing other kids over and jeering at them. Well, I simply wasn't that type. My sister took a bit of stick at first, too, and although she's two years younger than me and was in a different class, we stuck together at break times and tried to avoid the sneering eyes. But by the end of our first year in Cornwall she'd made a few friends and I wasn't being bullied so much, so life became a little easier.

One of the good things about the school was that it overlooked open countryside, where there were usually buzzards and kestrels flying around. The school was an ideal hunting ground for both these birds. They hovered over the playing fields and even sat on the goal posts. The bit of marshy ground beyond the playing fields was vole country, which was what attracted the kestrels. The surrounding fields were full of rabbits – the buzzards' favourite food – and from their perch on the goal posts they could spot a rabbit three or four fields away.

From a distance, a buzzard sitting on a post looks just like an extension of that post, because its brown plumage mingles very easily with similarly coloured items. Close up, of course, you notice that its feathers are very different from the colour and texture of the wood. A buzzard's feathers have almost a glossy look to them, and they're more than one shade of brown. If you observe the bird from the front, you'll see that it ranges in hue from the creamy white of the breast and stomach to quite a dark brown with even darker flecks on

Common buzzard

the neck. When the buzzard is in flight, cream is the main colour you see, and if you have good eyesight and know what you are looking for, it's quite distinctive, even from a distance.

Buzzards will eat much smaller prey than rabbits, particularly in the winter when food is scarce. They'll go for small birds, insects and even worms – but then, it's said that there's as much protein in a decent-sized earthworm as in quarter of a pound of beef, so it must be nourishing, if not very appetising by most people's standards!

Watching a buzzard in flight is very similar to watching a glider – it just seems to float effortlessly. It flaps its wings a few times to lift itself off the ground, then simply rises up, using whatever thermals and air currents it comes across. Every so often it will flap again to give itself a little more power and lift. I also used to compare the buzzard to a kite, being allowed to gain height gradually and seeming to grow smaller and smaller until it went out of control and soared off into the distance with the wind. I always noticed how the pale, flecked breast and dark bands on the brown and white wings faded into each other as the buzzard rose higher and higher. Eventually it was just a dark dot way up in the sky, almost unrecognisable except for the distinctive flight pattern: it would glide round in a circle, then soar off in a straight line, helped along by the wind, and finally resume its circular flight again.

As you watch a buzzard quartering the ground, it's easy to think that they are very lazy birds. But I'm always reminded of a large bomber aircraft coming in to land, moving very much more slowly than you'd expect for something of its size. The fact that the buzzard's soaring flight looks easy doesn't make the bird any less powerful.

You can tell the buzzard is a soaring bird by its wing shape, which is very much the same as that of an eagle. The wings are very broad and thick at the base and the feathers at the end of the wings are parted like the fingers of a human hand. The tail is also very broad and looks a bit like a Japanese fan when opened out fully. These two distinctive features are, of course, there for a reason: they allow the bird to capture much more air, which gives it a much better pushing force as it gains height. The principle has been borrowed by engineers for the design of the wings of large aircraft.

In summer the school air space was invaded by squadrons of swallows with their flashy stunt-flying. Actually, these intricate displays were simply high-speed insect-snapping flights. Swallows were everywhere. They nested under the guttering and I spent many a happy lunch-hour wandering around counting their grenade-shaped nests, made of mud and stuck to the eaves of the school buildings. I always tried to work out how many mating pairs we had. (Not all the nests were occupied, so this was trickier than it sounds.) Droppings, feathers and, sadly, dead chicks, littered the school premises. Sometimes I found it impossible to concentrate on my school work as the activities of the bird populations outside kept grabbing my attention.

'Is there something interesting out there, Jon?' a teacher would ask.

'Er – no, Miss.'

'Then why do you keep looking out the window?'

Someone would usually answer for me: 'Oh, he's watching the birds again, Miss.'

At which point everyone would crack up with laughter and I'd slide slowly down in my chair with embarrassment.

The teachers soon started to realise that I had this huge fascination for birds. It must have shown up in art lessons first. Whenever I had a sheet of paper in front of me and a paintbrush or pencil in my hand, the result was inevitable. A bird would materialise, crudely drawn at first, but always very detailed. My art was far from perfect in those days!

Thank goodness the teachers encouraged me, and I was allowed to express my passion in countless writing and drawing projects and models. My drawings often ended up on the classroom wall. But they put their foot down when it came to maths and they caught me grappling with the colour scheme of a kestrel.

All the painting and drawing I did at Tintagel Primary culminated in my 'masterpiece', of which I was quite proud. It was an enormous poster of various garden birds which I was asked to do for the school office. And there it hung until long after I'd left to go to secondary school in Camelford. Sadly, the last time I saw it, which was some years ago, it had pretty well faded beyond recognition. Perhaps by now they've asked some other budding young artist to do a new painting for that wall.

Out of school, of course, I continued my birdwatching just as I had done back in Essex, only now there was much more variety.

Whenever I could, I went out, armed with my expensive binoculars, to see what I could find in the fields or to observe the coastal birds – puffins, with the splendid red, yellow and blue bills which they shed when the mating season is over; cormorants nesting in colonies on ledges in the cliffs; screeching gannets and all the members of the gull family.

The puffin must be one of the most unusual of all British sea birds and there is something very comical about the way it moves and looks. Its brightly coloured bill and large head make it seem a bit top heavy and the small black tail looks out of place in comparison to the bulky body.

The first time I spotted a puffin I thought I was seeing things. Apart from its bill, at a distance it looked very much like an out of place penguin. In flight, its little wings look as if they can barely hold it in the air. I always think it would fit in as well in the Mediterranean as in the North Atlantic, because it has the black and white colouring common among all sorts of species of northern bird, and the brightly coloured bill and feet typical of birds that live in hot countries.

The cormorant is a browny black bird with a very distinctive glossy effect on its feathers. From a distance it looks more black than brown and it has a most interesting tail which, when closed, looks like one of the flippers scuba divers wear. It is very tall and can sit as still as a statue. It has a very long neck like a duck, and the front of the body sometimes has a faint purple tinge.

Its pointed head has the sort of bill you'd expect to see on a prehistoric bird with a notch at the end like an aircraft's radar. But beware. As I got older and people used to bring me injured birds to look after, I was always very careful of them and didn't approach without the leather glove I wear when working with birds of prey. Cormorants can be pretty nasty with their beaks. I once found an injured one walking along a beach near where I live, and when I picked it up to see what was wrong, I underestimated the length of its beak. It immediately grabbed my nose and twisted it round as it would have done with a fish. My nose started to bleed and my eyes streamed with water. Needless to say, I haven't trusted a cormorant near my face since.

Two distinctive features of the cormorant are a patch of white feathers where the legs meet the body, and another area of white extending from the rear of one eye under the head to the rear of the other eye.

Gannets amaze and impress me every time I see them. I think of them as the sea-bird equivalent of a peregrine or other member of the falcon family. The reason I say this is that they dive just like a peregrine, folding their wings and plummeting like an arrow into the sea to catch their prey. They fly through the air with extraordinary ease and in flight they are very distinctive – they have very long white wings with black tips and the tail looks more like a pointed piece of feather than a proper tail.

When gannets are on the ground, you can't miss the yellowy orange band of colour on the top of their heads which reaches down the back of their necks, and the unusual blue-grey hue of the beaks and feet. They also have a distinctive blue band round their eyes, which is surrounded by black feathers. The body is mainly white, so that from afar they look just like a large seagull. Young gannets are brown, very much like young seagulls, and have white cheeks.

One day when I was out in the fields, I even spotted a peregrine falcon high up on one of its hunting trips. In flight these birds are spectacular to watch. This one just hung there like a kite on an invisible string and then fell on its prey like a stone, somewhere in another field. The victim might have been a crow, a jackdaw, a pigeon, even a pheasant, but it wouldn't have stood much chance against the peregrine's talons. As peregrines have been known to dive at a speed of 180 miles an hour, they hit their prey with such force that they often break its neck, and sometimes even break the head clean off.

The adult male peregrine is a very distinctive bluey black in colour when seen from the rear. The front is even more striking – white with very strong black bands from side to side, becoming larger and thicker the further down the body they are. The beak has a characteristic yellow band, and there is a black band progressing downwards from the eyes. Their feet are also bright yellow and they have very large toes, each ending in a black talon. The wings are pointed, light in colour on the underside, like the chest, with a gradually curving pattern of specks. The tail is short and blunt-looking.

The female peregrine is slightly larger than the male, more brown than black, and the bands across the chest aren't as distinctive. The

Cornwall

You can see that ours is a bit of a mad house. Me with Dawn, Mum with Jasper the cat, my sister Leanne with Zara the kestrel, now deceased, and little sister Annamarie with Barry the guinea pig. Sabre the dog was old and ill when this picture was taken, and sadly had to be put to sleep shortly afterwards.

Owl Light

BELOW Dawn and I used to watch a lot of television while I was training her, but she was always easily distracted – she's obviously much more interested in what the photographer is doing. Now that her training is complete, she doesn't sit on my fist so much, but prefers the back of the chair or the top of the door. I don't know what she thinks about television, but she seems to enjoy the music on the car radio whenever we're going to lectures.

RIGHT This is the main stem of the wing feathers where the two parts of the wing overlap. Underneath are the primary feathers which are harsher and used for steering; the secondary feathers are on the top and used for catching the wind and for balance.

BELOW RIGHT A close up of Dawn's very soft head and neck feathers. The softness is a characteristic of owl feathers and makes for silent flight.

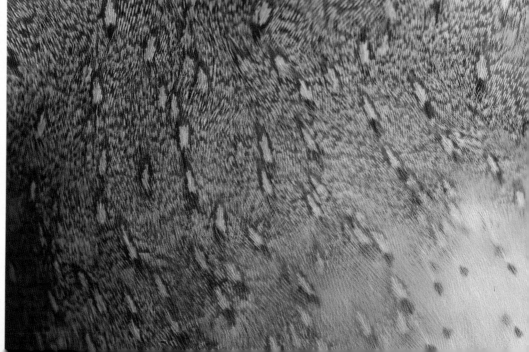

LEFT Dawn eating a chick, which when she was in training would be all she had to eat all day. If I'm not keeping her appetite sharp for flying, she has two or three chicks a day. She can easily swallow one in one go, so mealtimes don't last long.

ABOVE This sort of bloated, eyes half-shut look is typical of Dawn after she's eaten. She makes a sort of crackling noise which I've never been able to explain: it may be contentment – or perhaps she's asking for more.

Owl Light

BELOW Dawn just coming off her perch, her wings on the downbeat, cupping the air to give her lift.
RIGHT Dawn 'throwing up' – yes, it really is called that – as she's about to land on my glove. Her talons are thrust forward ready to grab the food.

The characteristic hunting pose of an owl quartering the ground or flying fast and low towards something it's spotted below it.

young are brown and lack the bands altogether, having white plumage with dark specks on the chest.

During the war, peregrines were declared a pest because they used to attack carrier pigeons and prevent messages reaching their destination. This led to a decline in numbers, but they are recovering, although the racing pigeon fraternity complain about them now!

In addition to their amazing dives, peregrines are capable of long, sustained flight. I've seen one at a display of falconry trying to 'creep up' on a pigeon. This isn't an easy thing to do, as you can imagine, and the pigeon took off. The peregrine chased it for six miles, and even then the pigeon did not give in. This wouldn't always be the case – the pigeon might be able to take cover and elude the peregrine, but the peregrine might equally decide that it wasn't worth the chase. It can't afford to expend too much energy on a prey it's not certain of catching. On the other hand, if the peregrine was flying high up, above the pigeon, it would have the advantage, because it could swoop down and break the pigeon's neck.

Another favourite haunt of mine was up at my nan's place, St Nectan's Glen, near Trethevy, a couple of miles from our house. It's very beautiful in the glen, like something out of a fairy tale, and there's a picturesque waterfall which is a major tourist attraction. Here I would see many interesting birds, but the most attractive to me was the dipper. A pair was nesting right next to the waterfall one year, practically underneath it. Their nest was a bit like an overgrown wren's nest – a pile of moss fixed on to the rock face. The dippers are browny-black in colour with striking, snowy white breasts; they're about the size of a well-fed blackbird, but far more enjoyable to watch. They are incredible divers, making perfect plunges into the foaming waters where the fall churns them up and disturbs aquatic life for them to feed on. They stay submerged for ages, until you begin to think you've only imagined you saw one go in – and then they pop up with a beakful of food. I've never measured how long they stay under water, but tourists walking along the path to the waterfall often report that they think a bird is drowning!

Towards evening the owls start up with their eerie hooting and screeching. The glen is a sort of spooky, secret place, said to be haunted by monks walking the Pilgrim Trail. I didn't venture further

Kingfisher

in to find the owls in case I bumped into a Brother. When I stayed overnight at my nan's, which I often did, I actually slept in a room next to where the old monastery used to be. As you can imagine, I didn't do much sleeping the first two or three nights I was there. Every time I heard the wind rustling in the bushes or rattling the slates I'd duck down under the covers, thinking of hooded ghosts stomping through the garden – or through the wall. And owls provided just the right sound effects for the horror-film atmosphere.

Owls call for a number of reasons. They may be trying to attract a mate, mapping out their territory, warning other males off. They are the only nocturnal birds of prey, and they stay awake most of the night. Even if they are half asleep, they will still be alert and ready to respond to any danger. Their eyesight is remarkable in poor light, so they hunt mostly at dawn and dusk. They sleep during the day, and you will sometimes see flocks of little birds mobbing a sleeping owl in broad daylight. These birds are the owl's potential prey, and they will fly around it, sometimes even peck at it, to disturb it and drive it away.

The whole valley round St Nectan's Glen is teeming with bird life, a paradise for a young ornithologist. Just below the glen the valley widens out into what is known as Rocky Valley, finally dropping off the map in rugged cliffs with a fall of some fifty or so feet down to the Atlantic Ocean. There are some ruins down there and some prehistoric engravings in the rock faces. It can be a pretty creepy place, too, but it's not as isolated and overgrown as the glen, so at least it's lighter.

Here I could inspect the nests of numerous smaller birds and their young. There were tits, wagtails, nuthatches, treecreepers – more than enough to keep any birdwatcher happy. The presence of all these species also meant that I had a good chance of spotting the birds that preyed on them.

There were, however, other predators in the area – the bird-watcher's menace, cats. One day I chanced upon a chubby black and white brute molesting a helpless young sparrow and rushed to the rescue. (I know that in wildlife programmes on TV the professional naturalists never interfere with natural savagery, but since the size of the moggy population in the area is unnatural, I felt it was right to lend a hand.) The sparrow wasn't too badly injured as far as I could tell, but it was obviously in a state of shock and couldn't fly. It needed care. Not knowing much about bird first-aid, I wasn't sure what to do, so I took the bird home.

I had heard that a couple who lived across the road from us, Maureen and Aubrey Edwards, took in and cared for injured birds. I didn't really know them – I'd been too shy to make friends with them, although I was interested in their work – but it was the only place I could think of. They were very helpful and admitted the patient immediately. I'd been right in thinking that he wasn't seriously hurt, and they soon had him well again.

That was the start of a long and warm friendship with the Edwards family. I discovered that they virtually ran a bird hospital and I was soon bringing them more casualties and learning a lot of useful things about bird-keeping and care.

On the whole, those first few years in North Cornwall were very happy times for me. After a while, the bullying at school didn't affect me too much, and I was in my element with all the wildlife around me. But then, in 1986, my father left home and my parents were divorced. This may have pushed me back further into my shell. I don't know. I've always got on well with adults, but it's only now that I'm starting to get on with my own generation, and I realise that I have to do that if I'm to become a whole person. But I suspect that the unhappiness at home threw me even deeper into my ornithology, and made me want to spend more and more time with birds.

One of the results of this was that I was often to be found across the road at the Edwards' place. From the street it looked like an ordinary, large, detached house. But if you looked carefully at the left-hand side, where there was a glass-enclosed porch, you might have noticed a few little birds flying around, the odd flash and flitter of coloured wings. And if there was a gap in the traffic and all was quiet for a moment, you might hear all sorts of weird twitterings, squawks, toowoos, cheeps and hoots.

Round the back you would step out on to a paved patio, leading to a long garden overlooking a field. But any flowers there might have been in the garden would probably have been eaten by the resident goats, rabbits and God-knows-whatever-else were around at the time, for the kind-hearted Edwardses never turned any sick or homeless creature away. Wild or tame, mad or sane, it was all the same to them. They just loved all animals.

But Maureen's speciality was birds. A lot of people thought of Maureen's house as 'the bird hospital', but in fact the garden was like a street of birds, with cages and aviaries stacked along either side of it like tower blocks. The patients who recovered in these boxes and enclosures came and went like the inmates of any other busy casualty ward, but, of course, there were big differences: most importantly, there was no waiting list, and no one had to pay! One day there might be a bleary-eyed buzzard with his wing taped up in a splint, looking very sorry for himself; the next there might be a baby sparrow basking under a red heat-lamp, recuperating from the attentions of a cat.

Unfortunately, despite all Maureen's efforts, few of these smaller birds ever survived such an experience. My sparrow had been lucky that I scared the cat off when I did. Mostly they died of shock, particularly the younger ones, so it was a bonus when one recovered. If only cat owners realised the damage their pets do to garden birds. Maybe if more people built high bird-tables instead of just throwing breadcrumbs out on to the lawn and tempting the birds to risk their necks, fewer birds would die from cat attacks.

Down the bottom of Maureen's garden there was a natural-looking waterhole (a muddy puddle, actually) for the ducks that roamed around wherever they pleased. They used to build nests in the hedge that divided Maureen's property from her neighbours'. A hedge is ideal for ducks to nest in – although they usually build their nests on the ground, using leaves and grass, they like them to be well hidden. So not only does the hedge provide the materials for the nest, it provides the camouflage as well.

One duck, however, wasn't a very serious mother – she would lay her eggs all right, but couldn't be bothered to sit on them long enough for them to hatch. Perhaps she had a poor memory and kept forgetting where she had left them. Anyway, it didn't seem to concern her – she would simply make another nest and lay some more. But as the drake plays no part in incubating the eggs, once the mother had wandered off, the eggs in the previous nests just went rotten.

There was one occasion when the addled eggs came in handy for pelting a kid on a motorbike who'd been riding up and down outside our house all evening and making a terrible noise. I distinctly remember seeing a few of the eggs hitting the spokes of his front wheel as he slowed down. The effect was very much like putting an egg in an open electric food mixer. The biker and his bike got absolutely plastered in a green slimy substance. Anyone who has ever smelt an addled egg will know just how horrible that would be. There was an unpleasant odour blowing along our road all next day.

One of the most interesting cases that Maureen came across that I knew of was a peregrine falcon. It was brought to her before I really got to know her, but it was with her for quite some time. Small wonder, too, when you hear what happened to it.

When I first saw it, it was hopping around in the bottom of one of the larger aviaries. It struck me as a bit odd that it never seemed to leave the ground. Strange behaviour for a falcon – they like to sit up high so that they can survey their kingdom. Then I noticed the reason for all this hopping and lurching. It only had one wing. Apparently every now and then it did succeed in reaching one of the lower perches, but I never saw it do so and to this day I don't know how it managed it.

I asked Maureen about this strange and spectacular bird, and she told me how it came to be in her care. Apparently it had been reported hopping about in a car park close to the village. When Maureen went to investigate, she discovered that the poor thing had lost its left wing. Obviously, this is a serious disability for a proud hunting bird like the peregrine falcon, but sometimes wings can be sewn back on. Maureen searched the immediate area, hoping to find the missing limb, but no luck. The cut where the wing had been severed was quite clean, and the blood had dried up, so she concluded that the poor bird must have flown through some overhead wires in the vicinity during the severe gales we'd had the night before. This is not an uncommon occurrence because birds of prey have what is known as 'tunnel vision' – which means that although they can focus with deadly accuracy on the prey straight in front of them, they have difficulty seeing anything outside that direct line of sight.

Well, there wasn't much Maureen could do about this injury, but the wound did heal up nicely and she cared for the bird for over a year. It didn't seem too distressed by life in the aviary with the other birds, although I imagine it was all a bit of a come-down for this once proud and merciless hunter of the skies. But eventually the Edwards

Peregrine

family moved down the road to run a residential home for the elderly (which, when you think about it, was a logical step from caring for birds!) and the peregrine and various other injured birds needed new homes where they could receive the same amount of care and attention.

So the peregrine was taken up country to a falconry and raptor breeding centre. As soon as it arrived, one of the staff thought there was something unusual about it, and he wasn't referring to the missing wing. After much investigation, he discovered that it wasn't a British resident at all, but a Russian bird that must somehow have been blown off course from its migratory route during the hurricane-force storms of the previous year – the storms that had immediately preceded its arrival in our village car park.

This happens surprisingly often with migrating birds – if the weather is too dreadful for them to be able to navigate properly (and they do seem to rely on the sun or the stars, like medieval sailors), they will land in the hope of finding food and shelter until the wind drops or the rain clears up. Which is why you find extraordinary things like a Russian peregrine falcon turning up in North Cornwall, when it might have been planning to spend the winter in the Tropics.

This story has a happy ending, because we learned later that the peregrine had been paired up with another Russian visitor of the same species. It might have been permanently grounded, but I'm sure it found life wasn't boring!

Although I was still barely into my teens when I was spending this time with Maureen tending sick birds, I learned a lot about general care and identification – even if we failed to spot our Russian defector. Watching Maureen feed very small birds who were unable to do it for themselves was to stand me in good stead later, when I began breeding barn owls. I remember the over-eager, gaping mouths and outstretched necks, as well as those who could only just about lift their eyelids and had to have the food forced down their throats so that they would have the strength to keep fighting for life.

The food consisted of seeds mixed with water, and various other delicacies, favourites of the particular species of bird – insects for the sparrows, caterpillars for the tits, nuts, of course, for the nuthatches. Meanwhile, the larger birds of prey were tucking into things like mice, rats, chicks and rabbits. We used to catch rabbits when we could, but Maureen bought the rest of the 'prey' from breeders who specialise in these things. Now that I have a number of birds of my own, I do the same. There's a hatchery in Ilminster where we buy day-old chicks by the thousand – my birds get through about five hundred every month or two. It's always the male chicks that are killed, as they're no good to the egg-producing farmers.

Force-feeding the birds of prey was sometimes necessary – any invalid may need to be encouraged to eat – though it is a dangerous business which I never attempted with Maureen's patients. But she was an expert and by watching her I at least gained some confidence, enough to feel I could try it myself one day.

Maureen's skill lay in basic first-aid and tender loving care, so I didn't learn about diseases or complicated injuries – but what I did learn was vital to my future work. I picked up a lot about different species and their habitat, simply by listening to Maureen talk about the lifestyles of the birds she was looking after. I also learned a lot of common sense about looking after birds – feeding them, keeping them clean, judging their general state of health from the look of them, that sort of thing. Seeing birds close up and handling them was a vital part of my education.

Before I met Maureen, it often seemed that for someone like myself, who was and is very interested in learning about all aspects of bird life, there was nowhere to go except libraries. And nothing you can learn from a book compares with what you can acquire through practical experience. I feel very lucky to have had someone like Maureen on my doorstep. Without her and Aubrey's help and guidance, I wouldn't be able to do what I do today. I owe them more than I can say.

By the way, I also grew out of throwing rotten duck eggs at noisy bikers.

3

Barny

By the time I was twelve years old I had been thinking for some time about getting a bird of my own. I appreciated I was taking on quite a responsibility – I knew it wouldn't be like having a budgie in a cage as a pet – but I felt I could cope. I wanted to train a bird of prey from scratch. Ever since we'd moved to Cornwall I'd been reading more and more about birds of prey, and by this time I was pretty sure that falconry was the ideal career for me.

Falconry has been defined as 'the taking of wild quarry in its natural state with trained hawks and falcons'. In other words, you train a bird of prey to do under your control what it would do naturally in the wild. It's one of the oldest sports in the world and was the 'sport of kings' in England long before horse-racing took hold. Nowadays, it's probably the only profession that enables you to spend time close to birds of prey and watch them in action.

There are falconry centres throughout Britain, but few of them are devoted exclusively to falconry. Most of them have a collection of owls and other birds on display to the public. Anyone who can train a suitable bird can set up a falconry centre, but the birds themselves are expensive to buy and to maintain, so it's not a hobby to be undertaken lightly. Some places run day courses – costing maybe £30 or £40 – where you can learn to hold a bird and fly it; they'd provide trained birds for the 'students' to use. But many centres insist that you take a four-day, one-week or two-week course. That way if you're really keen you can learn something worthwhile – and if you're just messing about you'll be put off by the price.

There's a lot to be said for the modern falconry centres – anything that helps people to appreciate birds of prey is a good thing as far as I'm concerned – although it's a shame they have to be turned into tourist attractions. I've discovered I'm a purist at heart and prefer the traditional approach to the sport!

But at the age of twelve I knew that a falconry course was way beyond my means, so for the time being I had to be content with reading about it. That didn't mean I couldn't acquire a bird of my own, though.

Unfortunately, as I said, my mother is allergic to feathers, so I couldn't have kept a bird at home even if I'd had one. I had a friend who was also interested in birds of prey, and we'd thought that we'd buy one each and keep them both at his place. My mother still said no, so I let the subject drop for a while. I just continued to read anything I could and watch avidly all the 'bird' programmes on television.

In the meantime, I became friendly with a neighbour, Derek Mills, and his wife Val, who said I could build an aviary on their land. This was not only extremely kind, it was very convenient, as our back garden virtually backed on to their field.

Derek and I built the aviary between us out of ordinary three by three timber and chicken wire. It's about twelve foot by ten foot, and seven foot high. In one corner we put a box where the bird could shelter, and we covered this with corrugated iron sheeting (though it's since been replaced with corrugated plastic). The box is screened so you can't see into it, giving the bird some privacy. At one end there are double doors, so that you can go in through the outer door and shut it before opening the inner door – which means there's less chance of a bird escaping. The wind has battered this aviary a lot and the wire needs replacing – in fact, when I can afford it I'm going to knock it down and build a new one, but it's been very useful over the years.

In the meantime, my thirteenth birthday was coming up, and it seemed like a good time to revive my request for the perfect present: a bird of prey.

As chance would have it, there was a couple living just down the road from us who kept animals – anything from horses to chinchillas, including a few birds of prey. Years later they even kept a black panther for a while, until there were complaints and they were forced to send it to a wildlife park. I decided to pay them a visit. They had a male barn owl who was about a year old.

To tell the truth, he didn't look in very good condition. His feathers were okay, but he looked overweight and unfit. This might have been because he'd been kept in an aviary and not given enough exercise, and I felt sure I could put that right. But I was in two minds about him for another reason: he was already too old for training purposes, and of course that was why I wanted a bird.

The younger you get a bird of prey the better, really – eight weeks is an ideal age. This bird had never been handled, so he was completely wild and had no human bond or imprinting (if you get a bird really young, it will think you are one of its parents, which helps). In fact, barn owls are reckoned to be one of the hardest breeds to hand-rear and train, and they aren't recommended for beginners – though I didn't know that then. What I did know was that I'd probably lost the battle with this owl before I'd started: I suspected he would be impossible to train, but I was so hooked on the idea of having my own bird that I could hardly drag myself away when I was looking at him. Despite my misgivings, I dropped heavy hints at home. I suppose I thought that I had to start somewhere, and if this bird didn't work I could always sell it and buy another. I didn't hold out much hope, anyway – Mum was still against the idea, and the aviary wasn't even finished.

I remember feeling a bit disappointed as I went to school on the morning of my birthday – I'd rather have stayed home and finished the aviary. The journey home seemed to take longer than usual because by that time I was dying to see what presents I'd receive. I was hoping for some money, as I was saving frantically to buy the owl for myself.

When I got home Mum was acting very strangely and frogmarched me off to Derek's house. She wouldn't give any explanation, so I assumed it was to collect a present that was too big to hide at home, like a bike or something. At Derek's we found a local photographer called Steve Blay waiting for us. He's a friend of the family, and although I was surprised to see him, Mum explained that he'd come to take a few photographs of me for the family album – after all, it's not every day you become a teenager. I swallowed this, and even as they walked me down the garden path and into the field where the half-built aviary was situated, I still had no idea what was going on. I feel a bit silly about it, looking back – I didn't even notice that the aviary had been finished, or that there was a tea chest mounted inside with a large 'front door' sawn out of it.

As we drew closer, everybody else slowed down and eventually stopped. I turned round to see why. I was standing with my back to the aviary, my jacket almost touching the wire mesh, still puzzled. Why were they grinning?

Suddenly there was a commotion behind me. I spun round to see what it was and was confronted by a barn owl flying madly around inside the aviary, flapping its wings against the mesh. I was dumbfounded. I honestly can't remember how I felt at the time – I think I was just shocked. For a moment I didn't even recognise it as the same owl Derek and I had been round to see a few weeks before. Derek had finished building the aviary by himself and they had bought the bird that very afternoon while I was safely away at school. It was literally a dream come true.

Derek, laughing heartily, gave me the key and I let myself in to meet my birthday present. I was so excited that I forgot I was going into a cage with a wild bird. There were a few frantic seconds while the owl went berserk around my head before disappearing inside its box.

It may not be very original, but I decided to call my own Barny. I thought it was appropriate, not only because he was a barn owl, but because if you say it fast enough it sounds like 'barmy', which he was a bit. It was also a simple name to shout during the training I hoped to carry out later.

I'd read a book called *Falconry and Hawking* by Philip Glazier, and I'd recommend it to anyone who was thinking of taking the training of birds of prey seriously. I knew that the first step was to introduce Barny to jesses. These are the leather straps you put round the bird's legs to hold it on the glove that you have to wear when you handle birds of prey. You also attach a swivel to the jesses and a leash to the swivel so that the bird is secure during short flights off your fist.

Always keen to do things economically if I could, I'd made my own jesses. Buckskin is recomended in the falconry books, but it's not readily available in this country and leather does the job perfectly well. You test the grain of the leather to see which way it stretches, and use the less stretchy bit for the length – otherwise it'll be like keeping the bird on a piece of elastic. Cut a suitable length of leather. This will depend on the size of the bird – you want it to be comfortable and to be able to move its legs, but you also want to keep an untrained bird under firm control. Fold one end of the strap over a couple of times and punch a hole through the three layers, then feed the other end through the hole to form a 'button'. Cut a slit in the other end of the jesse so that it will fit through the swivel, and punch a hole at either end to stop it splitting any further. The button end can then be fitted to the ring on the bird's leg, and the slit end to the swivel. (Any bird you purchase will be ringed. Almost all British birds of prey are classed as endangered and you have to have a licence to keep them. You also have to ring a bird that is to be sold, taken out in public or showed. Ringing is normally done when the bird is eight to ten days old.)

The two jesses – one for each leg – join the swivel in a V shape. The swivel is a device of two metal rings linked by a swivelling stem. It stops the jesses becoming twisted, and it also gives you something strong to attach a leash to. The swivel will turn with the bird's movements, so that it doesn't get caught up in the leash. When a bird is sitting on your fist, you keep the leash wrapped round the fingers of your glove so the bird's movements are restricted to the length of unwrapped leash. At the moment I'm training a red-tailed buzzard and only letting it move a few inches – just off my fist and back again.

Anyway, my worst fears about Barny were confirmed the first time I tried to put a leash on him. The result was disastrous. As soon as I managed to put them on him – which wasn't easy! – he tore away at his legs like a thing possessed and ripped off most of his lovely white leg feathers in the process. His flesh was red and raw, but even after wounding himself like that, which must have been pretty painful, he didn't stop. I'd been applying a special cream to his ankles which was supposed to harden the skin, but it didn't seem to do much good. I think he must have eaten a lot of it, though if it tasted anything like it smelt it must have been vile. He carried on ripping and tearing at his legs relentlessly and with sickening ferocity, even drawing blood at times. In the end I saw that there was no way he would accept this treatment, and that it was doing both of us more harm than good. I removed the offending items, and before it had really begun Barny's training programme came to a permanent halt. I gave up. You just can't teach an old bird new tricks.

However, I hadn't finished with Barny yet. He was to play the leading role in my plans to breed owls for release into the wild. Like the one-winged Russian peregrine, Barny was destined to become a father many times over. I put him out to stud, as it were. And very good at it he was, too, although he was a little over-enthusiastic, especially where young females were concerned. At one year old he was the ideal age for breeding and although he'd never been with another bird before, his first mate produced eggs within two months. As the incubation period can be anything from twenty-eight to thirty-six days, with twenty-nine to thirty-two being the norm, Barny must have worked out what was required of him pretty quickly.

A barn owl usually lays an egg a day or every other day until there is a clutch of four to six. So a week or so may elapse between the first and the last eggs hatching. Breeders can increase production by taking an egg away and putting it in an incubator to hatch. The female will then lay another to take its place. If you do this several times in the course of a clutch being laid, you can more or less double the number of chicks. The birds hatched in an incubator can then be hand-reared or given back to their parents, who will rear any number of chicks as long as they have enough food. Hand-reared birds can be put back in the nest once they can feed themselves, but if they've become imprinted on a human, they may not respond properly to the other birds and the parents may reject them.

Once a chick bred in captivity can fly – at the age of eight weeks or so – it can be taken from its parents and released to hunt for itself for a month. The idea is that it is then recaptured, but it will now be streetwise, so to speak, and good to train for hunting. Of course, this practice runs the risk of losing the bird, so it's not often done.

In captivity or in the wild, the first two clutches of barn owl chicks often die because of the parents' inexperience. An adult owl of either sex may kill its chicks and eat them – I don't really understand why, because they are known to do this even if there is plenty of food. I guess an inexperienced parent just doesn't know what to do with these intruders in the nest, and disposes of them the only way it can. In theory, the parent owls share the workload of rearing chicks. The father goes and hunts to bring back food, which he then leaves with the mother. It is her responsibility to feed the chicks and keep them warm – she rarely leaves the nest when she has tiny offspring. This obviously means that the male's workload more than doubles, as he has to hunt for his mate and the babies as well as himself. If food is scarce, the mother will feed the smaller, weaker chicks to the larger ones, to ensure that at least some survive.

Barny may have been a natural for breeding, but he was useless at actually rearing his offspring. In fact he was downright dangerous and ate some of the poor little things. It's easy when you become attached to birds to think of them in human terms, particularly if you give them a human name. But you've always got to remember that they are in fact extremely barbaric creatures. A bird of prey lives for food – it is the single most important thing in its existence. A bird kept in captivity is fed all year round, so obviously it has an easier time than one in the wild which has to feed itself whatever the season, but it still has the hunting instinct. When you look an owl in the eyes, you don't see wisdom, like folk tales say, you see cold, cruel pools – you see death. They don't have morals or manners, and they are not cuddly. To them you are just a very large creature who for some unknown reason feeds them, and for that, and that alone, they may give you a grudging sort of respect, if owls have any idea what respect is. I don't know why Barny chose to eat his own chicks, but I mustn't judge him in human terms.

Having said all that, owls are still lovable and I do kid myself that they care about me. And when I got Dawn, I did sense that I had formed an almost human relationship with her. I'll never know.

4

Dawn

When I realised that Barny was untrainable, I knew I would have to find a hand-reared owl if I was to stand any chance of training one successfully. As I said, part of Barny's problem was that he'd never had any contact with people at all, and by the time I got him it was too late. But I had my heart set on training a bird. In addition to the excitement of watching such a magnificent creature in action, it really is the only way to learn about birds of prey – and it would be my first step towards becoming a professional falconer one day.

So began my search for a suitable bird. Still unaware that barn owls are notoriously difficult, I thought that although my experience with Barny had been unsuccessful, to say the least, I should stick to the same breed. Also I didn't have much money, and barn owls are much cheaper than a lot of birds of prey. This is because they're no good for falconry proper – you can train them to fly free and return to you, but as they're nocturnal it's difficult to train them to hunt under 'controlled conditions', particularly if you want to do displays for the public. For this reason, they don't command the high price of, say, peregrines or buzzards, which the professionals prefer. Barn owls are popular as pets, though, and a good breeding pair can produce four clutches of eggs a year in captivity, which again keeps the price down – it's all a question of supply and demand. (In the wild, a pair's capacity to reproduce is limited by the availability of food, and one or two clutches a year is normal.)

I started looking in *Cage and Aviary* magazine after Sue Yen – the lady I'd bought Barny from – told me about it. I took it regularly and pored over it every week for two months, but search and phone as I might, I couldn't find a decent barn owl. Some breeders I rang didn't have any left, others didn't have any chicks of the age I wanted (and after Barny, I was very wary of buying anything more than a few weeks old), and others lived in the Highlands of Scotland or somewhere equally inaccessible to me. In fact, nearly all the breeders are based round the London area, which would still have meant a difficult journey to collect a bird, even if I could find one.

It was all terribly frustrating. I was so eager to start training an owl, I felt I knew what I was taking on, and yet the right bird eluded me. But then I had one of my rare good ideas: why not try ringing up those breeders who had only advertised at the beginning of the breeding season, about six months before? So I rounded up my bird-fancying friends' old copies of *Cage and Aviary* and studied them until I got back to the very beginning of the season, early March. I reasoned that this was where I would find a small breeder advertising his or her first clutches of chicks for sale – someone who wasn't big enough to justify advertising all year round.

In fact, although the breeding season is normally said to begin in March, this depends very much on the weather and, again, availability of food. Both in the wild and in captivity, a pair of barn owls can breed all year round if the weather is good and food plentiful. At Paradise Park, a sort of bird zoo near Penzance, a barn owl chick hatched on Christmas Day last year.

Nowadays I keep huge lists of every person, organisation and publication connected with birds, so I hope I'll never again have the problems I had finding that owl. But my hunch proved right, I came across a few likely looking names and phone numbers and eventually I found a breeder in Bow, East London, who had several barn owls, all brothers and sisters, who would be the perfect training age for me. In fact he had about eighteen birds on his books at the time, ranging in age from two weeks upwards, and he was hand-rearing them. This was very promising indeed and Paul, the breeder, sounded like a really nice, caring sort of chap, so I told him I was very interested, and would call with a definite answer in a few days.

Now I had the difficulty of how to collect the owl. I wanted a bird in the hand, but this one was practically in Shepherd's Bush! Derek was always very supportive of what I was trying to do – helping me build the aviary in his back garden had made him interested in birds too – but I couldn't expect him to drop everything and drive me from Tintagel to London. He had a business to run and he was up to his neck in carpets all day long; he's a carpet fitter, so you'll know what I mean. Finally, on the day that I'd promised to ring the breeder back and let him know one way or the other, a miracle happened – one of those strokes of luck that seem to come along when you least expect them to.

I'd gone across to the old folks' home to have a chat with Maureen and, inevitably, I was telling her about the trouble I was having. Well, it happened that Maureen and Aubrey were about to set off on a round-Britain motoring holiday. Maureen was very interested in buying a bird for herself, too, so she said, 'Ring him back, Jon, and get all the details. Tell him we might have two and I'll pick them up on our way back.'

I couldn't believe my luck. I dashed straight back up the road to my own house, rang Paul and told him I'd definitely have one, and maybe two. I explained about Maureen calling round to collect and said she'd bring the cash. He was obviously satisfied that I was on the level and reserved two birds on the spot, £35 each.

I waved Maureen off the next day, telling her I couldn't wait to see her again, that I would be counting the days till her return. Now all I had to do was wait.

Well, it was like waiting for Christmas when you're a small child: every day seems to last about six months. And the Edwardses were gone three weeks! Every day after the first two weeks I would look anxiously up and down the road, hoping to see their car. All sorts of doubts clouded my mind. What if the dealer had a cash-in-hand offer from someone else and went back on his word? What if Maureen couldn't find his house? What if there was only one bird left and Maureen claimed it as hers? No, I knew she wouldn't do such a thing. I was becoming paranoid. I was desperate. Why didn't Maureen come home?

I needn't have worried. At the end of the third nerve-jangling week there was a knock on the door. I can't be sure what my face looked like when I opened it and saw Maureen on the doorstep, but I imagine it must have had a grin on it from ear to ear. She was just standing there beaming, holding this big ball of fluff in her arms. The ball of fluff had an old hag's face in the middle of it, with two slowly blinking eyes and a huge hooked nose. At the other end were its feet and tail. The tail was just a stump with a few feathers beginning to show through, rather like the beard stubble that appears when someone hasn't shaved for a couple of days. The feet were massive in proportion to the tiny body. The heart shape that is characteristic of a barn owl's face was just beginning to show through. It looked really ugly and beautiful at the same time.

Maureen had bought two owls – this female, and the female's

brother for herself. She'd called him Sage, and she only stayed at my house for a few minutes as she had to get right back to see her new baby – the owl, of course.

It was obvious from the moment she came into the house that Dawn, as I'd immediately christened her (after all, I'd had three weeks to dream up the name), was a real character. I took her to my room, so that her feathers wouldn't get up Mum's nose. But I think Dawn must have known about her allergy, because the moment Mum came into the room to see her, Dawn made a point of trying to sit on her breasts. See what I mean about her being a real character!

I'd particularly wanted a female barn owl, because they're slightly larger and stronger than the males, and with the extra grey colouring or toning of their feathers, I think they're more attractive. It's purely a matter of personal preference, but as I sat on my bed that day, stroking Dawn, I knew that she was the one. The whole business had been getting me down. My dreams of training an owl had come to a standstill with Barny, and then another standstill when I couldn't find a bird to buy. But now at last I had one, and she was my heart's desire.

I was just so relieved. The longer my quest had gone on, the more Mum had begun to react to my moans of frustration with reservations of her own. She knew that I'd have to keep Dawn in my bedroom to start with, and she'd been beginning to have second thoughts about letting me do that. Luckily, the moment she met this cute little owl she came under her spell and fell in love with her, too. They were never to become what you would call bosom friends, however, because every time Dawn went to Mum for a cuddle, Mum would sneeze and send her flying beak over tail across the room. And Dawn's downy feathers got into everything, no matter what I did. She was continuously moulting as she grew her feathers, and however many times I hoovered I could never get it all. In the end I gave up.

So it wasn't quite a fairy-tale ending, but we did all live more or less happily ever after. And as you'll see, Dawn proved to be a remarkable student, passing out with flying colours. A real little princess, you might say.

When I first got Dawn she was a little over three weeks old. I kept her in my bedroom for another three weeks, so that Mum wouldn't have an allergic reaction. I wanted to keep her warm and handle her as much as possible in preparation for training. Occasionally I would take her into the lounge and Mum would have to keep back and hold a handkerchief over her nose and mouth so that she couldn't smell the feathers. (Have you ever tried having a conversation with someone who is holding a hanky over their face?)

At the time I couldn't bear to be parted from my new little owl. I was so proud of her that I wanted to take lots of photographs of her while she was young, just like a proud parent with a new baby. But I couldn't get my camera to work – I hardly ever used the thing – so I went to Derek's house one day to ask his advice on how to operate it. I couldn't even put the film in properly! When I arrived, I found to my great irritation that I'd forgotten the film. I'd been a bit dithery for a few days, sort of clumsy and absentminded, as you often get when you're feeling under the weather.

Well, after a while – this was around nine in the morning – I decided to go back to my house and get the reel of film. I only live a few doors down the road from Derek and normally it would have taken me just a minute or two, but on this occasion it seemed to take ages. I remember picking up the film and making my way back to Derek's, although even now the memory's a little hazy, and then I started to feel light-headed and dizzy. Val, Derek's wife, noticed immediately that there was something wrong. She saw that I was looking pale and vacant and told me to sit down. I did as I was told and flopped down on a chair, but it gradually got worse and worse, and I felt as if I was going to be sick. Also, when I went to stand up I was so whoozy that I just couldn't keep my balance, so I slumped back down again.

'This boy is very ill,' I heard Val say.

'Growing pains,' said Derek.

'Don't be so daft!' said Val. 'Call the doctor.'

The doctor was called. I was now drifting around in my own head, although I did see my mother rush in. She was obviously flustered and I'll never forget her concerned eyes staring into mine. From then onwards I deteriorated fast. I had been moved into the front room and laid out like a corpse on the sofa. Squiggly things were swimming round in front of my eyes, like transparent tadpoles. I couldn't move a muscle, my whole body felt like jelly. I'd gone stone cold but felt boiling hot. It was like a fever, sweat was pouring out of me. The doctor arrived and after examining me pronounced that I had some sort of mystery virus, and there was nothing he could do for me. When I heard him say that, I thought he meant I was going to die. I tried to get up but Derek's firm hands pushed me back down. Then I heard the doctor, as he was leaving, say something like 'Keep an eye on him . . . I'll call back later . . .' I smiled with relief.

Next Derek came up with the bright idea of making me walk to see how far I could get. The women protested, but in a moment I was upright and swaying around. I reached the floor pretty quickly, even with Derek's strong support. By now I was virtually paralysed from head to toe. I could just about twitch my fingers, but certainly couldn't pick anything up. My arms were hurting and felt like lead.

Derek had another inspiration: what I needed was fresh air. I was promptly carried outside into the garden and propped up in a chair. But I did not perk up, so they carted me back indoors and called the doctor once more. The same one came back, looking a bit annoyed. He kept banging my leg with his little rubber hammer to test my reflexes, but there was no reaction. He still couldn't get to the bottom of it. Meanwhile, I was sweating and burning up so much that I was in danger of melting away into a puddle.

I am very vague about what happened during the rest of that morning, but apparently Val, Derek and Mum wanted a second opinion, so another doctor was called in. He took one look at me and said, 'Hospital.' I was in another world by this time, inhabited by see-through creatures resembling owls and parrots; it was a sweltering hot day and I was turning into a pond to support a dying race of transparent tadpoles. I was definitely hallucinating.

Somebody phoned an ambulance and was told that it would take between an hour and an hour and a half to arrive, so Derek volunteered to drive me to Casualty at Freedom Fields Hospital in Plymouth, forty-five miles away. Later I learned we made it in just under an hour, although I don't remember a thing. When we got there I was immediately admitted for observation. No one had a clue what was wrong with me and I had no idea what was going on. I was in hospital for five days but I don't remember anything about that, either. Mysteriously, a nurse later said that one night I got out of bed and walked to the toilet, and yet the next day I couldn't move. I have no recollection of this night-trip to the loo.

After two or three days I started picking up. I don't know what medication I was on, or whether I ate – it's all a blank. Amnesia is a weird thing; it's like I lost five days out of my life. Finally, my father came and I was discharged and taken home. I spent about a fortnight in bed, and then felt fine again. Thankfully, nothing like this has ever happened since.

The funny thing is no one knew what I was suffering from. It might have been a delayed reaction to the drugs I had been taking for an operation I'd recently had on my foot, but this seemed unlikely. After much speculation we all started to point the finger at Dawn. I read about a kind of pneumonia owls can sometimes get, which humans, too, can catch. It's a bit like psittacosis, the infectious disease parrots suffer from, which they can also pass on to humans. Had I been infected by my owl? One night before I went to bed I asked her. There was no reply, but just as I was turning away I swear I heard Dawn sneeze.

One of my next purchases is going to be a book on veterinary aspects of birds of prey. My local vet is really helpful, but he's not a specialist, so I hope this will help him, too!

5

Training Dawn

The first stage of Dawn's training was to make her sit on my fist properly, which meant getting her used to people, and to wearing the jesses and swivel and everything that had caused Barny to go berserk. For about three weeks I sat constantly for about four hours a day with Dawn perched on my fist, watching TV or listening to the radio, quietly trying to make it seem as if this were the most natural thing in the world for a boy and his owl to be doing. Even if I went into my bedroom to read or do homework, I'd still have her sitting there on my huge falconer's glove, fidgeting and glaring at me.

Encouraging her to tolerate the equipment was quite difficult at first. She'd be very antagonistic when I was putting the jesses on, so the first thing she would do when I picked her up was pull at her feet and try to work herself loose. She'd been used to hopping around and flapping about wherever she pleased, so it came as a bit of a shock to find her freedom of movement restricted by the jesses. There was a look of betrayal in her small, moony eyes, and as I looked into them I couldn't help feeling a sense of guilt. I just had to keep telling myself it would all be worthwhile for both of us: one day she would be flying free, which is not something that always happens to birds of prey bred in captivity.

For the first few days, Dawn would pull at the jesses with her beak every ten minutes or so. During this time she gnawed her way through two sets of thick leather straps and ruined most of her leg feathers into the bargain by continually ripping them off. Barn owls' leg feathers go right the way down to their feet, which makes them much more vulnerable than, say, a falcon, which has scaly skin on its legs that toughens up very quickly during training. No matter how careful I was, Dawn soon had raw patches of skin where she'd pulled out her feathers. I had to apply antiseptic cream on a couple of occasions when this pulling and rubbing with her beak had actually caused some bleeding.

The other great problem at this stage, of course, was getting her

Dawn

used to people. Within about ten days she was happy enough with my mother and sisters around, but it took her a lot longer to settle down with other people, and with animals.

When she was fastened to my fist people really scared her, whereas if she had been free she would have been able to take evasive action. If we were sitting in a room and someone came in talking or making a noise, Dawn would panic and it would take me a few minutes to calm her down. If a door creaked she'd jump with fright. Even less familiar sounds upset her, but then barn owls do have excellent hearing – they can hear a mouse moving on a woodland floor during a gale-force wind.

One of the functions of their facial disc is to transmit sound to the ears. Barn owls have one ear slightly higher than the other, so sound comes to them at two different pitches. When they hear something that sounds like prey, they move their heads until the frequency is the same in both ears, then keep their heads exactly in position and fly straight towards the sound. As they close in on the prey, they thrust their talons forward and the mighty claws take over. Owls' eyesight is good in dim light but not so good in total darkness; it is their acute hearing and the accuracy with which they can pinpoint sounds that make them such successful hunters.

Dawn's nervousness while she was attached to my hand lasted for quite a while and there was nothing I could do about it other than reassure her. I just had to be patient, it was one of those things. The bird has to get used to its surroundings gradually. Slowly but surely, however, she started to appear happier with the new arrangement. By the time I'd had her a fortnight, and she was about five weeks old, her trust in me was growing.

The family pets were more difficult. Birds and cats, as everyone knows, do not normally hit it off, and when Dawn met our cat, Jasper, this was most definitely the case. For about a week cat and owl kept out of each other's way. I don't think Dawn liked the look of Jasper's claws, and the feeling was mutual. The atmosphere around the house was pretty frosty what with Dawn's long, cold looks and Jasper's icy stares, so I decided to start introducing them formally. I put two chairs together, sat down on one with Dawn and got my mother to sit on the other chair with the cat. The bird, of course, would fan out her feathers in typical 'threat' behaviour, to make herself look bigger and fiercer. She would hiss, cluck and even stick out her tongue – anything to deter the cat from doing whatever it was she thought the cat was plotting to do. Jasper, on the other hand, would sit there stiffly, with his ears pricked up, eyeing Dawn and apparently thinking, 'Well, shall I or shall I not?' But luckily he kept his distance and never quite found the courage to have a go at her. And if I'd been in his skin, and seen the power in Dawn's beak and feet, I don't think I'd have done anything either.

There was to be very little thaw in this cold war, but amazingly our family dog, Sabre, started to get quite friendly towards Dawn. He was an Alsatian/Labrador cross and Dawn, perhaps because she could see that he was just a big, overweight softie and no threat whatsoever, dropped her defences and began to relax in his company. In fact, within a week I could sit on the same chair as the dog with Dawn on my fist. Sabre would simply ignore her and nod off, while Dawn would, as usual, sit there tugging at her jesses. It took another week or so for the cat to start to ignore Dawn, and even longer for her to stop taking too much notice of him and actually watch TV. She always observed every move he made out of the corner of one eye, though, and if he stirred in any way, even just to stretch or yawn, she would immediately react and flex herself to take defensive action.

Although it might sound as though Dawn was petrified of Jasper there were a number of occasions when she scared him out of his skin. Once Dawn took it into her head to attempt a sudden flight, jumped up in the air and found herself agonisingly caught, because of the tenderness round her feet under the jesses. The result was a frenzied sort of screeching aerial war dance. Poor Jasper happened to be curled up asleep some five feet away at the time and was rudely awakened. He, in turn, leapt about three feet off the armchair and made a lightning bolt for the door, which unfortunately was closed. It was like a Tom and Jerry cartoon to see him bang his head on the door, bounce back, look a little dazed, and then remember the terrifying 'nightmare' he was escaping from, and shoot for cover behind the sofa. Luckily my mother was out of the room at the time, or Dawn and I might have been sent to our room for giving her precious cat a heart attack.

One of the main processes in training a bird, and one which gave me a few problems, is known by falconers as 'manning'. Basically, this is getting the trainee bird used to strangers and strange surroundings. This meant that I had, from the beginning, to spend a lot of time with my family while Dawn was learning to sit on my fist. You will appreciate there isn't much point in training a bird to do this if every time you enter a different environment or a stranger comes into view it becomes hysterical. This process can take anything from a few weeks to a few months. It probably isn't worth persisting much longer than that, because if a bird doesn't respond by then, it's never likely to. The problems I had getting Dawn used to my family were made worse for two reasons. First, my mother's allergy meant she would sneeze every time she came near the owl, and, secondly, my little sister was so fascinated by Dawn that I couldn't keep her away. You can imagine what loud sneezes did to Dawn's nervous system and how dangerous it is to have a playful two-year-old near a very jumpy bird of prey! My other sister, who was just coming into her teens, showed very little interest in her big brother's 'crazy' owl, but kept her distance, rather like a rabbit, I thought.

Visitors were probably the biggest problem of all, for people calling round didn't expect to find a barn owl sitting in the living room. Some of the neighbours knew about my interest in birds, but they thought I kept them in cages. Their initial reactions were natural enough: they'd start pointing or gesturing towards Dawn and their voices would automatically grow louder through surprise and excitement. They would also move closer to have a better look. Dawn's reaction, too, was natural: she would start to get ruffled, then agitated, then threatening. The visitor would understandably back off quickly and there would either be pandemonium or an utter, stunned silence. At that point Dawn and I would usually have to leave the room.

Eventually Dawn settled down and began 'ruffling up' her feathers. This means fluffing them out and adapting them to whatever atmosphere she found herself in, and is a sure sign of contentment in a lot of birds. Others display their feelings of relaxation by standing on one leg, as you've probably seen flamingoes do in nature films.

A barn owl's body feathers are mostly for warmth, while the wing and tail feathers are used for flight. There isn't much body under the feathers, so it's vulnerable to rain and damp, though the feathers are a good protection against the cold. The soft down absorbs water like

ABOVE The facial disc of barn owls is the most clearly heart-shaped of all the owls. It encloses the beak and eyes and helps transmit sound to the super-sensitive ears. Again, you can see the beautiful soft texture of Dawn's feathers.
BELOW Four young barn owls at different stages of development. The youngest, on the left, is about four weeks old; the eldest, on the right, is fully fledged at nine or ten weeks. The hag-faced look of the very young mellows by the time the chicks are about six weeks old.

You'd be amazed the things people want you to talk about at lectures! This is a way of showing what an owl's pellet looks like when it comes out of the bird, and then 'dissecting' it to show the various bones and other indigestible bits and pieces that pass through the owl's system.

Dawn is very special to me, but I always have to remember that she is first and foremost a wild creature. These feet are designed for catching and killing.

Zara the kestrel, sitting on my glove with wings held out, tail fanned out and head bent down in typical hovering pose – she suspects I have food somewhere.

LEFT The red-tailed buzzard that I've started training recently, eating the leg of a rabbit. These birds come from America, so they are difficult to get hold of and I had the added problem that I was looking at the end of the breeding season. I was supposed to be saving up for a car, but I'm still too young to take my driving test, so I bought her instead – with the first payment of the advance for this book! She had been trained to hunt and then not used, so I've had to start training her again. She's about seven years old, fully mature, and might live to be thirty or thirty-five. A fully grown red-tail is a massive bird, over two feet tall – this one looks me in the eye when she sits on my fist.

ABOVE A father barn owl bringing food to his mate and chicks. Unfortunately if anything happens to the mother he seems to be incapable of passing the food on to his offspring. (Dennis Green/Bruce Coleman Ltd)

A quarry on farmland near where I live. Barn owls roost during the day in the main tree in the picture, and tend to fly out between the bushes on the right.

a sponge. An adult owl normally knows this and stays in shelter, but inexperienced hunters may not have the sense to come in out of the rain. Then they become waterlogged and are unable to fly until they dry out. They may also catch chills. I've heard of owls drowning in cattle troughs because they dive in to bathe, not realising how deep the water is, and become too wet and heavy to get out. They have also been known to attack their own reflection in a mirror, so the sight of an imagined owl in the water may be another motive for diving into a trough. There are other reasons for owls not hunting in the rain – it hampers both vision and hearing, and limits vole activity, too, so there's less prey even for those owls that do choose to venture out.

About a week after Dawn first started 'rousing up', I felt she was ready for the next stage of her training. I had to start introducing her to people and places outside the home environment. This presented a hazard that she hadn't experienced before – traffic. Our house is just off the main shopping street of Tintagel, so there is always a lot of traffic going by. Cars and lorries hooting, accelerating and braking put Dawn into a real flap. I decided the only thing to do was throw her in at the deep end and go right down the village high street, where the roads were busiest and noisiest with holiday- makers, and simply stand there trying to calm her down. Of course, I would only do this in the evenings when the streets were at their quietest.

The effect we had was really amusing. We'd be sitting or standing, watching the traffic go by, Dawn alternately flapping about desper- ately trying to get away and perching on my glove letting me stroke and soothe her. Cars would slow down so that their drivers could have a better look. Sometimes we literally stopped the traffic. Friends would walk by, too, or stop and talk. All this was really good training for Dawn, as it was contributing to her becoming accus- tomed to being a 'captive' in the noisy world of humans.

This stage of training an owl is much more difficult than doing the same stage with a falcon, because with a falcon you just stick a hood over its head and let it get used to all the different noises. An owl's head is too big and feathery for it to be 'hooded' or blindfolded satisfactorily, so the problem of 'manning' is twice over – you have to acclimatise it to both sound and vision. And barn owls are very inquisitive, as I discovered later when I began to take Dawn out into the fields. She was easily distracted by any noise, particularly if there was a chance it was food or another bird calling, and this sometimes made it difficult for me to make her concentrate on what I thought she should be doing.

After a week or so of being outdoors Dawn gradually accepted the sights and sounds around her. When a car went by she'd simply track it with her eyes and remain fairly unruffled; stirred you might say, but not shaken. She might even turn her head right round to see where the car had gone, but she wouldn't consider it important enough to jump off the glove. It would now take a motorist burping their horn or a dog barking nearby to get her hopping mad, which was real progress.

However I found there was always something new to overcome. For example, just walking with her could be troublesome. If there was a stiff breeze and a lot of traffic about, she'd become what is called 'wingy'. This refers to her opening her wings fully and riding the wind. Obviously it is not to be encouraged when you're walking along with a bird on your glove, because the first thing that happens is the bird takes off. A barn owl isn't strong enough to hold tight to a glove in a strong wind. At the moment I'm training a red-tailed buzzard, which is a much bigger bird, and its claws are strong enough to allow it to grip on to my glove, so this isn't so much of a problem.

In the wild, an owl would find shelter if it was too windy, closing itself up as tightly as possible. Alternatively it might use the wind rather than fighting it: it would allow the wind to lift it up and then come down, flapping its wings and 'closing down' until it was able to drop. But if you're walking along with a bird on a jesse, your movement disrupts it and stops it protecting itself from the wind as it would do naturally. So Dawn would have to fly off a little, giving in to the force of the wind, and then come back.

The only way around these attempted take-offs was to walk very slowly so that we didn't build up too much ground speed, as airline pilots would say, and stop if Dawn's wings did open. If I stopped I found that she'd immediately close them again. We must have looked a comical sight in those days: a boy and a bird 'dancing' up the road – two steps, stop, turn, two steps, turn, stop . . . Gradually, by walking slowly and shielding her from the wind as much as possible with my body, I cut the wings-open time to a minimum.

Our outdoor training sessions, however, could still be spoiled by hostile dogs, which would sometimes lunge at us from garden walls or charge round corners. I'd have to spend half an hour calming Dawn down after these attacks. But I was determined to get her ready for anything we might meet in the great outdoors. Our sessions increased. Sometimes I spent up to six hours a day with her, just getting her 'streetwise'. It was starting to get on my mother's nerves; she thought I was spending far too much time with the bird and not enough with human beings! I suppose I was in danger of becoming a sort of 'owloholic', but I was thoroughly enjoying myself. All I was doing at this time, if I wasn't at school, was watching TV, listening to music, reading or walking, with Dawn as my constant companion. And when I wasn't with her, like when I had to go to school and she had to stay behind in my bedroom until I came home, she was all I could think about. I wondered what she was doing, if she was all right, what I'd do with her when I got home . . . I think I even dreamed about her at night. It wouldn't be an exaggeration to say I lived for that owl during that very intense period of training.

Even at school I'd slip her into conversations whenever I could. Not all my school friends believed I was training an owl, so when they said things like, 'What're you doing tonight then, Jon?' I'd say, with a wicked grin, 'Oh, I'm spending the evening with me bird.' Of course, they'd immediately jump to the wrong conclusion and think I was talking about a girlfriend, and I'd get some almighty teasing, but the joke was on them!

Of course, there was a more serious side to all this. It was true: I was spending every evening and night with my owl, so I wasn't leading what could be considered a normal teenager's life. I realised I was missing out on things like girls and parties. When friends asked me out I had to turn them down and one or two of them stopped calling round. In effect I'd cut myself off from other kids of my own age. But this couldn't be helped if I was serious about training Dawn, which I was. I found it a bit disturbing sometimes but I just had to accept it. It was a necessary sacrifice. How could I expect my friends to understand that training a bird was virtually a twenty-four-hour-a-day job?

However, quite a few teachers took an interest in what I was trying to do, especially the biology teachers, who were impressed with my knowledge of birds and conservation, and my English teachers, who soon heard all about my interest because whenever we had to give a talk in class, I would launch into a full lecture on rearing and handling owls and other birds of prey. They would ask me how the training was going from time to time and this interest spurred me on. One of the English teachers, Frank Almond, who was keen on filming, even videoed Dawn shortly after I'd trained her to fly free.

Once I'd accomplished the first stages of training, getting her to sit still on my fist, I had to move on to the next stage: getting her to feed there. This was absolutely vital if I was ever to 'fly' her, because it would be the lure of food on my fist that made her come back to me. It would have been impossible to get her to eat if there was the slightest bit of tension in her. All birds are very temperamental and finicky with their food at the best of times, so I started by slipping titbits of chick under her feet while she was sitting on the glove. The aim of this simple exercise was to get her to move her feet and become aware that there was something tasty right under her beak, as it were. First of all she just ripped at it and slung it around, although after a couple of days she was tearing off dainty morsels and swallowing them. But she was still only playing with her food like a bored baby. I overcame this problem quite easily in the end: I just gave her less for supper when she was off my hand, got her weight down, say, half an ounce, and built up her appetite, so that when I had her on my fist she'd be hungry. After about a week she was tearing off big lumps of the dead chicks I was feeding her. Then I realised this was unusual for an owl, because in the wild they tend to swallow their prey whole, so I simply stopped holding on to the chick and soon she was gobbling it up in one. This she did rather neatly by picking it up, tossing it in the air and catching it in her throat; it was like a party trick.

So I succeeded in training her to feed on the fist. Teaching her to do this when she was moving, however, was a different matter altogether, yet another stage in the patient, painstaking training. And you can't hurry patience.

If a bird has food, it's much more concerned with what's going on around it, because it's afraid that another predator might steal it. You may even have noticed this alertness from observing the behaviour of the domestic dog: they're much more wary when they're eating. So encouraging Dawn to feed when we were out of doors was not as easy as it sounds, because her attention was completely absorbed in what was happening around her. Again I had to resort to cutting down her weight, so that she'd be hungry enough to focus more on the food. But I had to be careful I didn't knock her weight down too much, because her fitness could deteriorate. Birds do not have large reserves of fat; in the wild they're more or less constantly at their perfect flying weight. A drop of over an ounce for a bird Dawn's size could have seriously damaged her health, and, therefore, her ability to fly. And I must admit I didn't know at the time exactly what her flying weight should be. While I was training her, I kept her weight at about $10\frac{1}{2}$ ounces. This was partly because it is easier to train a bird to come back to you if it's hungry – not starving, you understand, but a bit peckish and more interested in food than it might otherwise be. Now that Dawn is fully trained, her weight tends to be about 12 or 13 ounces, and that's fine for her. During training – or later, if I wanted to knock her weight down for any reason – she'd have one day-old chick a day. Even now, two or three a day is all she needs. Birds in the wild don't have much variety in their diet – it really doesn't seem to bother them – but I give Dawn mice sometimes, and a rat every now and again as a 'treat'. She has a rat on top of the living room door on Christmas Day, for example, and it will last her two days. It's too heavy for her to carry, so she pulls it to pieces with her beak, holding it tightly in her talons. It's all very messy. (My red-tailed buzzard, on the other hand, can drag a fully grown rabbit in her claws, but then she is two feet tall and weighs 3 pounds or more, nearly four times Dawn's weight.)

Something I found distasteful at first was the actual preparation of Dawn's food. I wasn't used to handling dead things, like chicks, not to mention mammals like rats and mice. I mostly use chicks I buy frozen from a local supplier. Although it has now become a way of life, I still find it disturbing. There's something about watching little birds, even dead ones, being torn to shreds by a powerful beak that turns my stomach. Obviously you get more used to it the more often you do it, but it's still pretty gross. Each chick you feed the owl feels like a little sacrifice. I could actually feel Dawn ripping up the dead creatures as she sat on my fist and the blood was soaking through my glove. It was a very sickly, unpleasant and sticky sensation. Truly gruesome. And then of course there was the smell. It was all very violent and distressing to observe at close quarters and the stench really brought it home to me. My mother wasn't too pleased either because sometimes there would be spillages on her carpets. Training a bird of prey is definitely not recommended if you've got a weak stomach and a house-proud mother!

There was, however, a funny side to all this, although it sounds a bit ghoulish to mention it. On one occasion I was round at a neighbour's house and despite my warnings that it could get rather messy, they insisted that I show them how Dawn fed. Sure enough, right in front of her astonished onlookers, she set about disembowelling a dead chick. I held out my free hand to catch the gooey bits before they fell on the rug and, mischievously I thought, Dawn proceeded to place them in a precise bloody pile in the palm of my hand. A few mouths dropped open and then there were a few nervous giggles. They were really shocked. Needless to say, I wasn't asked for a repeat performance!

There were many other incidents like this one, some even more distasteful, but I'd better not go into them. The point I'm trying to make is that you can train a bird of prey to do only certain things. You can't house-train it as you can a cat. You can't teach it to eat from a certain bowl in a certain place, or to do its business in a litter box. The whole idea is to get the bird to act naturally on your fist. After this, of course, you reach the last stage of training: free flying.

This stage of the training took place in the field beyond our back garden. The object is to train a bird to fly free, but then to come back for food. I would have the food in my hand – hence all the effort to make her take food from me at home – and I made sure she could see it, however much I loosened her leash. In the end, of course, the theory is that the bird gets used to the food being there and comes back at the wag of a finger.

Of course, once you release a wild bird, however well you've trained it, you do run the risk of it just flying away. I think it's more likely to happen on the third or fourth flight, once the bird has caught on to the idea of freedom, which is why it's important to keep it reasonably hungry. Dawn did once disappear for two days, but I now know where to look for her if she vanishes. There are various likely barns near where I live where she might seek shelter, and I've always managed to lure her back with food. Sometimes it's worth going away for a while and letting her think she's beaten you, and then coming back with the food a few hours later.

I also know how to get the red-tailed buzzard out of a tree at night, so if it flies off I stay by the tree in which it settles until dark, then I go and fetch sticks and a torch so that I can see what I'm doing. I can literally push the bird out of the tree into a net or a box so I can take it home, because it can't see to fly off in the dark.

The sophisticated way of tracking birds is by telemetry. You attach a transmitter to the jesses and keep the receiver with you – this can pinpoint a bird within a hundred yards over a radius of fifteen miles. And if you're flying more than one bird, you can take the transmitter off when you've finished with one and simply attach it to the next. It has disadvantages, of course: bigger birds like eagles tend to bite the transmitter off, and, like so many things to do with birds of prey, telemetry sets are expensive. For the time being I'll continue to rely on knowing enough about a bird's habits to be able to track it down.

I found I had to get Dawn's weight down much more than I'd expected, or would have wished, just to persuade her to come for the food on my fist. To begin this stage of training you have to get the bird to step on to your glove, not jump, but step, very deliberately and confidently. And that is not easy. You have to be sure the bird is very hungry, and if it's not you have to sit down and wait for a long, long time. Over the first four days it was all I could do to get Dawn to step off the perch I'd set up in the field, with my glove just a few inches away from her. Sometimes she'd keep me waiting there for over an hour while she scanned the surroundings through 180 degrees, over and over again. I imagine it would be virtually impossible to sneak up on an owl.

When she did finally reach for the food, or lure, all she would do was lean over and rip off a piece, rather than step on to the glove. I started moving the lure when it was already in her beak, but before she could tear it. Then she had to make that all-important first step. If I took the food away from her too often, though, there was a danger she would lose interest, so I had to give in to her a few times. I couldn't let her have her own way every time, however, otherwise she'd end up training me! It was really a battle of wills. Quite often she'd make a grab, I'd move with her and there would be a tug'o'war, ending up with the food breaking or her giving up. When this happened she had one option; there was only one other perch available: my fist. It was either that or dump herself on to the perch in a heap, having given up the struggle, and she was much too graceful and proud to let something as undignified as that happen.

She soon discovered that by stepping on to the glove she had the food literally at her feet. Whenever she did this successfully, of course, I'd reward her handsomely with more food and words of praise. Birds, like people, will not waste their energy. It waasn't crucial at this stage to get her to step on to the glove repeatedly; it was more important for her to develop the right attitude to the whole process. I had to make her see that the exercise was worth her while. You just have to carry on making the bird think about the reward, until the step or jump becomes automatic. In Dawn's case, it took a full week before she was 'jump flying' the full length of her leash, from the perch to the glove. I had now accomplished a vital part of her training process. She was ready for the next stage of free flight!

With most birds, unless they're very stubborn, if you increase the distance between perch and glove, little by little, they will readily fly the extra distance. You wait until they're looking your way and then give a whistle or call. I could see Dawn thinking to herself, 'Oh, well, this is easy.' And then she'd make the jump and glide to my fist. As long as I ensured that she was in peak physical condition, it wasn't too difficult to get her to fly further the next time. To do this, of course, you have to put the bird on a much longer line, something falconers call a 'creance'. The one I used for Dawn was a hundred feet long.

To begin with I tried a loose creance. Basically, you hold this as you would a short leash, wrapped around your bottom two fingers and tied to your glove, so that you can easily pay it out as you increase the flight distance. I allowed about six feet at first, just in case Dawn overshot the glove. The problem with this was that although Dawn was interested in the chick, once she was airborne she also realised that she had freedom and that's very attractive, too! So she'd try to fly to another perch, which is what you call in falconry 'fence-hopping'. And obviously this must be discouraged. The whole point is to get the bird to come back to you every time.

To prevent her flying off I used what I called a 'straight creance'. This consists of a long line tied to one perch, which the bird is sitting on, stretching across the field to another perch, up to 120 feet away.

I then attached a ring to this line and connected it to Dawn's leash. She would have the length of the leash to fly with, but would only be able to fly in a straight line, to me, at the other end of the fixed creance.

At first Dawn would attempt to continue beyond the far perch where I was waiting, instead of landing on my glove. This was only natural, so I just had to grab her leash as she flew by and carry her back on my glove. After a while she began to get the message, but it required a lot of patience. It was five weeks before she would regularly go for the chick along the line, and even then she'd often wait for up to ten minutes to make up her mind.

The problem with the 'fixed' or 'straight' creance, however, was the wind. Dawn preferred to fly into the wind, to use the updraught, and then angle in at my fist. This was fine until the wind direction changed slightly and came across the fixed line. She would then try to adjust her flight path to the fist by altering direction into the wind. Of course, the short leash would not allow her to do this. It was at this point that I decided to put her back on a loose creance, so that she could approach the lure from whatever direction she pleased. I had to give her a little reminder now and then, to stop her attempting to fly off into the wide blue yonder, by gently pulling the leash, but within two days she was coming to me just as willingly as she had on the straight creance. I still thought she should be keener, however, so I knocked yet another half an ounce off her flying weight, until she was so eager that she set off towards me virtually the moment she saw me putting on the glove. We were now at a crucial point in the training. She was getting tired of the equipment – the leash and ring and creance – slowing her down, and I had to pluck up the courage to let her fly free for the first time.

I invited Richard, a local falconer friend of mine, and his girlfriend Rosie to come over and watch Dawn's first flight. I wanted Richard's opinion on her flying ability. He and Rosie were both impressed by the loose creance work I was doing, so I took a deep breath and removed all the equipment, except for the jesses.

For Dawn's first solo flight I played a little trick on her. I set her down on her usual perch and slowly walked in a straight line to the far perch, some ninety feet away. If my deception worked, she'd still think she was attached to the creance and fly straight to me as usual when I showed her the chick. There were a few anxious moments, but as soon as I pulled on the glove she came straight at me, low and very fast indeed, much swifter of course than she could have done if she had still been carrying the equipment. It was breathtaking. Even Dawn must have felt good about it. She must have realised that she was no longer encumbered, but completely free. She had never flown so fast and with such ease before. I flew her three times straight off, and then returned her to the aviary.

I felt an incredible sense of relief and achievement, but as Richard quickly reminded me it's not during the first free flights that a bird takes the opportunity to fly off, because it doesn't fully realise what it means to be free. It's when you've been flying them for a few days consecutively that it (pardon the pun) dawns on them that they could escape and find out what's over the next hill. I still had that hurdle to overcome.

This is something else that is more difficult with an owl than a falcon. Falcons are interested in food to the exclusion of everything else, but an owl likes to know precisely what's going on around it, even if it's hungry. So the first thing an owl will do when you release it is to scout out the land. Dawn is particularly inquisitive, and I soon discovered she would never fly properly in a new area without investigating it first, even if I was holding out food for her. Not only this, but because owls are naturally nocturnal, if I released Dawn during the day, she was quite likely to seek out a suitable roosting place rather than come back to me for food, if the fancy took her. As a result, I was often wasting my time during our first few flying sessions.

As I was training Dawn more to display her than to use her to hunt, this comparative lack of interest in food wasn't a problem. Later I trained a kestrel which I found much less inquisitive and more likely to come straight to me for the food. I'm training the red-tailed buzzard as a hunting bird, though, and I've found it sometimes prefers to look around for food for itself, rather than just come to my lure.

After Richard reminded me of the problems I was about to face following that first flight, I wasn't looking forward to the next flying lesson. Just for a moment my glorious sense of achievement faded into apprehension.

I had ideal flying weather over that first week, though, and Dawn was soon flying distances of 250 feet from perch to fist in Derek's field. It was at this point, partly because I was so nervous, that I felt it necessary to build her weight up a little, so I fed her up and overdid it, with the result that she got above her ideal flying weight. I had to wait four days before I could risk flying her again. If she wasn't hungry enough to be interested in food, she could easily have flown off. My nerves were really on edge when the time came round to try her, because I feared she might have lapsed, forgotten how to fly to me. So I did something you shouldn't really do after a bird has completed a successful free flight: I put her back on the creance. She knew what had happened, all right: she was being slowed down again. On her first flight the drag held her back. She flew well, though, so I removed the creance after just one flight. This time she seemed to be in two minds about what to do. There was an agonising delay as she pondered.

As you can imagine, I was really nervous again. I couldn't take my eyes of her. I could see her checking out every point on the landscape, sussing the locality. What would she do? It must have only lasted a couple of minutes but believe me it felt like hours. Suddenly she rose from the post, some 250 feet from me, and with a dozen or so leisurely beats of her magnificent wings she was angling in to land on my glove and devour her prize! I sighed with relief and quickly snatched up her jesses, wrapping them securely round my bottom two fingers.

'Good girl, Dawn,' I breathed, 'good girl.'

It took me a few minutes to feel brave enough to try her again. This time she more or less flew straight to me, and I felt confident enough to fly her another three or four times, each one successfully, although eventually I sensed she was losing interest, fretfully tearing at her jesses and gazing round. I was concentrating too hard to feel elated or amazed that I had actually trained this wild creature to come to me at will. That sense of achievement would come later.

I knocked her weight down an eighth of an ounce in preparation for the next flight, but the next day the weather was too bad for flying, so I 'fattened' her up again. We're talking about half an ounce, which doesn't exactly sound like a weight problem, but it took me another day or so to take it off her. Meanwhile the weather had not improved at all, setting me back several days. I never fly the birds in bad weather, which means sometimes Dawn goes two weeks without a flight. The red-tail can cope with fairly strong winds, but

Dawn can't. I give them extra food when they're not flying, because there's no need to keep them even slightly hungry. In the wild, a barn owl would take refuge in a barn and would probably manage to catch mice there. Failing that, it can survive on spiders.

At last the rain held off and although the wind was a little strong I knew that I had to fly her. Once more my nerves were frayed. But I needn't have worried, she came to me just as smoothly as before, and I flew her half a dozen times a session over the next four days. We had both come a very long way.

When you're training a bird, however, there always seems to be yet another step. After three weeks of perch work I decided it was time to start training her to fly from other locations. In other words, she had to go off and find places for herself and then fly back to me. I didn't want to have to keep carrying her back to the same perch for the rest of her life, although she did occasionally fly to the perch herself, she was so used to it. Now the old problem arose again: she found herself in new places and she was more interested in exploring them thoroughly than she was in the chick, even though she was at flying weight. I knew she had to come to me each time, it was just a case of sticking it out. Once she kept me hanging around for an hour and a half, which might sound like a backward step, but you have to remember she was sitting in a place of her own choice, and was taking it all in. Anyway, after I'd introduced her to a few different locations and got her over the initial newness of the experience, she seemed perfectly willing to come to me. At this point I thought I'd cracked it, and I probably had, but even now each flying session is a nerve-wracking experience, at least for me!

Everything I've said about the training of Dawn might lead you to think it's just a question of patience and keeping her weight at the right level, but there really is much more to it than that. Even when she was flying to me from various positions, the slightest disturbance in the landscape might distract her attention. And often she'd touch down on my glove only to find something not quite right and promptly take off again. I had to keep calling to her and whistling and showing her the chick. It was exhausting. The whole process was one of the most tiring and yet satisfying things I have ever done in my life.

And still there is something more needed in order to train a bird. There were times when my temper was sorely tested. Our relationship was rather like that of a father and child. You have to love the bird. You have to give your whole self. Really. One of the most touching moments in the whole training period demonstrates this point, and it is just one of many special instances I can remember. Once, during free flying, Dawn disappeared in some long grass. I called and whistled and waited a full hour and a half. No Dawn. Finally, I was forced to walk over to her – and no self-respecting falconer likes to do this. I was feeling pretty angry with her as I stomped across that big field, but when I reached her my heart just melted. She had flattened the grass, burrowed down and made a cosy little nest for herself. And there she was: sound asleep. I just laughed, but it brought a lump to my throat too.

Sometimes, when she was startled or frightened on my fist or as I approached her, it was painful to think that I might be responsible for her fear. And that's what it's all about really: a loving, trusting relationship. Without that there can be no training. I don't know how Dawn really feels about me, whether love or trust mean anything to her or not, but I do know that there is something special between us, and it feels like something more than just conditioning. I couldn't have trained Dawn if we hadn't felt this closeness or warmth for each other, and you can't learn how to build such a relationship from books. You have to experience some sort of bond between yourself and the bird, something almost unfathomable but nonetheless real. Dawn and I, I like to think, have such a relationship.

Man has been training birds of prey since ancient times and I am in no doubt that success has always been based on patience, mutual trust and observation. If anyone wanted to attempt it from what they've read in this book, I would strongly recommend that they think very carefully about it before they acquire a bird. I know of one boy who tried it and lasted only fourteen hours! It's extremely time-consuming, and if just one step, a single link in the chain of training, is missed or rushed, the whole process is ruined. In my case it was all worthwhile, but then Dawn is not merely a pet; she is a wild creature and always will be. She's also very special and there isn't another barn owl in the world like her!

6

Lectures

When I was in the fourth year at school we had to do orals as part of our English GCSE examination. We all had to stand up in turn in front of the class and give a short talk, followed by a question-and-answer session. The idea was to assess our ability to present a speech, paying close attention to vocabulary, non-verbal communication (body language and tone of voice) and keeping a sense of what the audience is thinking. Little did I know how useful these things were going to be to me in the future.

Quite a few of my classmates had done their speeches and I was getting really nervous as the day for my turn drew closer and closer. At the time I was in the throes of training Dawn and it seemed obvious that I should do my talk on the owl. My teacher, Mr Taylor, did tell us to do our talk on something we knew about, so I asked if I could bring Dawn in and tell the other kids about what I was doing. He thought this was a great idea and suggested I structure my talk in two parts: the training of Dawn, and a little bit about barn owls in general. I didn't know very much about barn owls at the time, so I busied myself reading everything I could find on them, in the library and magazines. It was pleasant work.

By this time Dawn was fully grown. Barn owls leave the nest at two to three months and are sexually mature at one year. They are capable of flight at 56 days – a strange figure which nonetheless seems to be remarkably constant. The oldest known wild barn owl lived to be nearly eighteen years old, but a male in London Zoo was recorded at twenty. In fact, remarkably few birds of prey survive their first winter in the wild, but once they have done so life seems to be a bit easier for them.

In adult plumage a barn owl is beautiful and Dawn was no exception. By the time I came to do my first talk, her feathers were a lovely tawny colour with large patches flecked with grey and smaller specks of black and white. The characteristic heart-shaped facial disc had come through an almost golden colour, and her breast was a stunning white except for the top which had a very faint tint of golden brown. The black specks along the side of her body are often found in female barn owls, but not so much in males.

From a distance her eyes are dark black but if you look closely you see a ring of dark brown around the pupil. The female barn owl is usually taller than the male, about 14½ inches to his 13, and also usually darker. This is not always the case, though – I once had a kestrel that I'd decided from its plumage was a male and it turned out to be a female, and although this has never happened to me with a barn owl, I know people who've made that mistake.

The big day for my talk soon came round. Derek gave me a lift in with the bird and all the equipment and said he'd stay with me in the classroom in case anything went wrong. I was grateful to him because I was really shaking with fear, so much so that poor Dawn could hardly sit up straight on my hand. Her feathers were rippling up and down like leaves in the breeze as she struggled to get a secure footing on me. Although she was trained, she was still a beginner – like me – and it wasn't easy to settle her down in front of all those kids, who, naturally, were all pointing and whispering when we came into the classroom. I'd get her settled and then there would be some distraction and she'd start jumping around, or 'bating' as falconers call it. I can't remember much about that first talk, but it went on for much longer than the five to ten minutes it was supposed to last. I just introduced her, said that she was a female and went on from there. I knew I was going on too long, but I kept thinking that Mr Taylor would butt in and stop me if he wanted to. He didn't. Every time I looked across at him he just grinned and kept his arms folded. The whole class was wide-eyed, glued to the bird. I don't think they were listening to a word I was saying, they were just watching to see what Dawn was going to do next. For them the time must have flown by, but for me it seemed as if I'd been standing out there all morning! Anyway, after about half an hour – the whole lesson – I just dried up and said something like, 'Well, that's it.' My ordeal was over. To my surprise everyone applauded.

Afterwards Mr Taylor kept me behind even longer, asking me more questions about the bird. I didn't mind because I didn't like the next lesson anyway. I'd done really well in the test, he said, gaining the joint highest mark in the class. As you can imagine, the news that Hadwick had an owl in school spread round like wildfire. I remember standing in the dinner queue and all these kids coming up to me, asking me if it was true, where I had got her from and what I was doing with her. I turned red with embarrassment. I simply wasn't used to all the attention, but I answered their questions as best I could. By then I have to admit I wanted to stop talking and get back to my quiet one-to-one relationship with Dawn. There was still so much to do. Besides, despite the fact that I'd got a good grade for my speech, I thought I'd made a bit of a mess of it and was just relieved it was all over. As far as I was concerned that was an end to it. But I was wrong.

Two weeks later, to my horror, Mr Taylor stopped me in the corridor and asked me if I'd consider doing another talk – to another class. Apparently he'd been telling all the other English teachers about it and now they all wanted their classes to see and hear about Hadwick's owl. Well, I could hardly say no, although it was the last thing I wanted. This time I was even more nervous. I mean it was one thing standing up in front of my own group and giving a lecture, but it was quite another kettle of kippers doing it in front of a strange class. I knew some of them and they were notorious. They would take the mickey out of me with sickening enthusiasm. I was paralysed with fear at the very thought of making eye contact with them, let alone playing the teacher. But three days later there I was, with Dawn perched on my fist, chatting to the whole mob. It was a nightmare for someone as shy as I was then. But I needn't have worried.

I was meant to talk for fifteen minutes but I went on for three-quarters of an hour. I wouldn't say I enjoyed it, but it went much better than I expected and my audience were very appreciative. I suppose it was a sort of novelty lesson for them. Anyway, I was congratulated once more and I realised for the first time that I was actually doing some good. I was telling my own age group about something worthwhile: bird life and conservation. It made me feel great – so great that I agreed to do yet another lecture, this time in front of a full fourth-year assembly – that's over a hundred kids! Oh God, what have I let myself in for, I said to myself that night.

When I did the first two talks, Dawn wasn't trained enough to fly, though on the second she did manage a short hop, but by the time this big lecture came along she was flying on the creance. So I intended to try flying her for the assembly, and carefully got her down to her flying weight. The event was to take place in the Music

Room, which is a large round building quite separate from the main school and connected by three covered walkways. It was just right: quiet, high-ceilinged, well lit, big and airy. (The air can get rather ripe-smelling in an ordinary classroom, especially when I start opening up and passing round owl pellets to show my audience what she's been regurgitating!) Well, when I arrived there they all were, sitting down waiting. As soon as I entered the room I could hear little pockets of chatter coming from various parts of the audience. I knew they were talking about me, and some of them were pointing at Dawn. It was really difficult to keep a straight face, but then Mr Taylor 'introduced' us and I just forgot about my shyness and launched into my speech. I'd already set up the perch, so I put Dawn on it as I spoke. I was becoming an old hand by now; I wasn't nearly as nervous as I had been the other times, even though the audience was twice the size. The adrenaline was certainly pumping, but I realised it was just a matter of getting over those first few minutes.

I kept them interested for half an hour and now I can't even remember what I said. It was all off the top of my head. I had some notes jotted down on a card somewhere, but I quickly went off them and chatted about whatever seemed interesting. (I've done dozens of lectures now, in front of all sorts of people, and I always make it up as I go along, although I suppose I must have a rough idea about what I'm going to say.) When I thought I'd run out of things to say I asked the front two rows to move back and the whole place started buzzing. It was Dawn's turn. They knew I was going to attempt a display. There was one kid, however, who didn't move back as far as the rest of his row, so I politely asked him to get in line. Well, there's always one. I suppose he thought I was exaggerating the danger and he'd show how tough he was, so he moved his chair back about an inch. I just shrugged and warned him to watch out, but he still didn't take any notice.

It took me three or four minutes to coax Dawn into a short flight. She overshot the glove and was pulled back by the creance. The second time she picked up the lure and pulled up clumsily on my fist. At this point I thought she might be distracted by the kid whose chair was sticking out, so I asked him for a second time to move back even further. Reluctantly he moved back but was still sticking out slightly from the row. I flew Dawn once more and this time she crashed down near this particular boy's feet. The next moment she was running up his outstretched legs, then flapping up his sweater and finally she was sitting inelegantly on his head. Everyone in the room burst out laughing – even the teachers. It was very comical, but the boy didn't think so. I'll never forget the expression on his face, it was like someone had shown him a ghost.

'Get her off – it hurts!' he whispered at me, not daring to move or make too much noise. I knew Dawn's talons would be finding a good grip on his scalp. Seeing as he'd been such a pain, I was a little slow going to his rescue. I laughed, apologised to the audience and walked over to lift her off. This wasn't easy either, because she was spooked and was clinging for dear life to the poor kid's hair. Eventually I untangled them and muttered something to him about it having been a hair-raising experience . . . He was not amused, although I think his pride was hurt more than anything else, but he did move his chair this time – right back into the second row!

I then flew Dawn successfully three times, just to prove she could do it, and brought the show to a close to a great wave of applause. I don't know how much they really enjoyed it, but judging by the expressions on their faces and the way they all went out talking about Dawn, I think it went down well.

I visited a few primary schools next. Again it was word of mouth: teachers told other teachers about us and I was getting offers to give talks left, right and centre. I went to Tintagel primary school a few months later. By then Dawn was flying free, although she wouldn't always come straight back to me. We were in the sports hall and she flew right up on to the top of the climbing frame at the far end from where I was giving my little lecture. All the kids found it highly amusing when I had to climb up and fetch her. Then she flew on to a high window-sill and I had to ask the headmaster to bring me a ladder so that I could bring her down. This was not part of the display, I hasten to add! Even when she crash-landed into the middle of them they found it funny. They were really 'wicked', those little juniors.

With primary pupils you get a lot of really complicated questions, and sometimes really good ones too. At one primary school I was asked a question that made the teacher look worried, and it baffled me. Out of the corner of my eye, I could see Derek thinking, what's he going to say? A little nine-year-old had just asked me, 'Jon, how do they do it?' I didn't know what to say, but I'd been reading about mating in a book only a few days before, so I kept a perfectly straight face and replied.

'Well, they do it in the normal way usually. But there is one bird – an eagle, I think – which actually does it in mid-air . . . Er, any more questions?'

The teacher and Derek both sighed with relief and the kid just looked amazed, as if he was thinking, 'What's he saying, I wouldn't have thought of that!'

On another occasion one child asked me why owls flew. You just have to give a straight answer. I said that owls couldn't run very fast and so they had to fly to catch mice, which *could* run fast. Simple answers like this seem to delight younger kids, who demand a reason for everything. But sometimes they ask things like, 'Jon, how many owls are there in the world?' They expect you to know exactly how many there are, even the exact number of barn owls in the British Isles, right down to the last check. You just have to say something like, 'Not enough,' and admit you don't know.

It's a curious thing, but at the end of a talk when you say, 'Any questions?', you don't get that much response from an audience. But afterwards, when you're packing up and taking equipment out to the car, you suddenly find yourself surrounded by pupils and teachers firing questions at you. I suppose people prefer to wait until most of the audience has gone. These cosy chats often last longer than the lecture itself, but I don't mind. Children have sometimes got personal things to say, like, 'We've got owls in our barn' or 'My uncle's got 'em on his farm' or 'What are they doing in my friend's shed?' So I ask them what the land's like, is there water? Does your dad use pesticides? Things like that. It's surprising how little even these country kids know about owls, although they must see or hear them every day. They learn a lot more at my talks, even though I'm just going over the very basics of the subject.

It gets a little more difficult when eight-year-olds who've seen me handling Dawn wander up and say they're going to get a barn owl and train it. Most of them think it's as easy as that and then I have to give them the 'hard facts' about cost and time. But – although this is very rare – you do sometimes come across one or two who seem to have a genuine interest and 'feel' for the birds; then, obviously, I try to give them all the advice and encouragement I can.

Sometimes these sophisticated nine-year-olds really do seem to have the bug but I still feel a bit uncomfortable encouraging them because they are so young. I mean, I've had my interest virtually since I was in nappies, but I didn't actually get a bird until I was thirteen. So I try to put the younger ones off acquiring one until they're older. They look disappointed, but I say study first, train later. It's difficult. I don't want to kill their dreams. The whole point of giving talks is to educate young people; tell them what's happening to our barn owl populations; give them some simple biological background; and talk about training. I don't want to say, 'Look, you're too young – forget it.' Those who have a real interest will leave it for a few years before attempting training.

Another problem with doing these talks is working out at what level I should pitch them for different age groups. In the beginning Derek was always saying things like, 'Don't talk about that', 'Talk more about this', or 'They won't want to hear about that.' But I'm the one who has to stand up out there and do it, and so while I take his point I have to find the right levels for myself. It's all trial and error, really. For example, I'm careful about using certain words, like 'frequency', with younger audiences, when I'm telling them about the owl's unusual 'lopsided' hearing. Some things are very tricky to explain. You can plan grand lectures, but in the end you really do learn by doing them over and over again, adjusting this or changing that. You soon sense if your audience is with you and taking in what you're saying.

The worst age group for me is my own, because I sometimes think they see me as a bit of a know-it-all. Well, I might know about owls but I wouldn't claim to know much about anything else. I remember I did a talk at Rudolf Steiner, a private school in Devon, to a group my own age and it went really well, so there are exceptions. I did make a big mistake there, though. I thought one long-haired kid was a girl but she was a he! Derek cracked up, but I was dumbstruck – super embarrassed – for about thirty seconds, and went as red as a radish.

Another time I went to St Kew primary, which is really small and right out in the middle of nowhere, and they made me feel really welcome. That happens a lot, but St Kew was special. It was raining cats and dogs and the teachers were running in and out helping us get our stuff in and just couldn't do enough for us. It's great to be appreciated. The teacher who'd invited us down proved very useful in helping us to locate release sites, too. The children had brought in a number of dead barn owls, so there was already a bit interest. We were there all morning and had a wonderful time. The teacher invited us round to his cottage one evening for dinner and to talk about releasing owls into the wild, which we had just started doing around that time (I'll tell you more about that later). The next day he even drove us out to some local farms in his Land Rover to assess their suitability. So doing the lectures not only benefits the children, it also makes me valuable contacts, as well as building up my confidence; I never had much of that until I started training Dawn. I can honestly say that every audience I've ever had has been very good, except, perhaps, for a school for the mentally handicapped we visited once where one or two started turning round and talking whilst I was speaking. They weren't being deliberately rude – it was just hard for them to concentrate. They were definitely interested, though. It was quite funny really and I enjoyed it very much.

As I said, I've done dozens of talks now at various schools, but one that sticks in my mind is a private preparatory school for girls in Tavistock, where I was received like some sort of pop star! There'd been something in the local papers about me and my work, and these girls, aged about eight to eleven years old, sent me a book of poems they'd written, printed and sold to raise money. The poems were all about owls and me! They'd raised £35 and sent it to me to put towards my conservation work. I was really touched, speechless. So on our way to the Rudolf Steiner school we called in unannounced to say hello and thank you.

You can't imagine how excited these sweet little girls were when they saw me and Dawn coming into their school. They went wild and made us promise to come back and give a display, so a few weeks later we returned and gave them the whole show. It was amazing. I'll never forget their hospitality and generosity. At lunch time Derek and I almost caused a riot in the dining hall, because between us we could obviously only sit at two tables at once and every table wanted us to sit with them. There just wasn't enough of us to go round! It was hilarious.

By the time we'd got out of there I'd received two 'love letters' from a couple of nine-year-olds and pocketfuls of poems and drawings. Derek really gave me some stick about my 'fan club' on the way home in the car; he told my mum everything, and she had a good laugh, too. But it was just a delightful experience. It's hard to describe how nice everybody was to us at that school.

A few weeks later I had a letter from them, saying another man had visited them with a barn owl, but it wasn't as good as Dawn. I felt very proud of her and read her the letter. As soon as I've got some suitable breeding pairs I'm going to go back there. I hope they read this book and realise how happy they made me feel.

Although I am still nervous at the thought of doing a talk in front of strangers, once I get going I enjoy every minute of it. The places I've been and people I've met have given me the confidence to carry on. I don't claim to be an expert and I certainly don't consider myself a clever clogs. I'm just someone who's into what he's doing. I simply love it. I sometimes think back to that first talk I did in Mr Taylor's class, and how scared I was. I owe Mr Taylor a lot. At the time I just wanted to be left alone, but now I'm glad he pressured me into doing more talks. It had never occurred to me that so many people would be interested in me and Dawn. It shows you how wrong you can be, and what you can do if you fight your fear and try. You might say I was learning to fly free, just like Dawn.

7

The Falconry Course

'Beware the falconer with the clean glove,' they say, and certainly I was looking forward to getting my glove dirty – at least metaphorically – with some practical experience when I booked myself on a falconry course on Bodmin Moor in the summer of 1988. I was still in the middle of training Dawn and she had just started to fly free. As I've said before, falconry has always fascinated me, and I hope I'm going to be able to make my living at it one day.

The course was important to me for several reasons. I wanted to learn as much as possible about different birds. People who don't know what they're doing can kill birds of prey – their weight is very delicately balanced, as you've seen from the trouble I had finding the right flying weight for Dawn. A kestrel is even smaller than a barn owl – it may only weigh six to seven ounces, and could easily lose a quarter of an ounce overnight in cold weather because of the energy it uses up trying to maintain its body heat. That's the equivalent of a medium-sized man losing half a stone overnight, and it could be fatal for a bird. So it's vital to understand just what the right weight is, and how to feed a bird to keep it fit but well fed.

I also knew that experience in working with other birds would be useful to me in the long term. Sooner or later I want to acquire the full range of British birds of prey, and the next bird I hope to work with is a goshawk. They're quite easy to train and hunt a variety of prey from small birds to pheasants and hares, which makes them interesting to work with. They have a tendency to be temperamental, but it would be good experience. The main reason I became involved in birds of prey was to teach them to hunt for me – and of course for themselves – so a goshawk is a must for the near future.

At the time I did the course I was still very inexperienced, and inclined to be impatient with Dawn's training. Dawn had at first been reluctant to get off my glove, so I'd developed the habit of swinging my arm with the wind, hoping to encourage her to fly. I'd read about this technique in my books, but it was only when I did the course that I realised that, although it would work for sparrowhawks and most other hunting birds, Dawn's hunting did not depend on speed. So instead of being encouraged, she was being buffeted about and becoming distressed. Now I know that if I hold my arm up but keep it still she has the benefit of the updraught and will open her wings and take off.

I arrived bright and early at Brian the falconer's house for day one of my course. Derek had come along too, to keep me company and because he fancied the idea of hunting with hawks. For me it meant more than that. It was the fulfilment of another personal goal I had set myself. So far I'd acquired all my know-how about birds of prey from books and first-hand experience. Now it was time to extend my knowledge with the help of a professional falconer. It was a necessary part of my education.

After we'd sat and talked in Brian's kitchen for a while, we were taken through to the falconry part of the house. It was a large room, an Aladdin's cave to any would-be falconer, filled with expensive-looking equipment: bags and lures hanging from walls, jesses and leashes all laid out in immaculate order. Right at the back, sitting stony-eyed on a perch, was a large buzzard. Our eyes met and all the while we were sitting down discussing what we had to do and how we were going to go about it over the four days of the course, my gaze kept returning to the sour-faced buzzard. If looks could kill . . . I tried to stare him out. Soon I'll be handling that magnificent specimen, I thought. I longed to feel the great buzzard's weight on my fist.

'Jon? Are you still with us?' Brian broke in.

'Er, um, yes, Brian. That buzzard, is he . . . ?'

'Pay attention.'

This induction session lasted about three-quarters of an hour, and then Brian took us outside, past the ever-watchful buzzard.

'Come on, Jon!' called Brian.

Derek laughed. 'He's in another world,' he said.

We all donned gloves and picked up a couple of Harris's hawks. These are handsome, rusty brown birds with a remarkably amicable disposition for a bird of prey, though they can catch a rabbit or a bird as large as a heron with ease. They are excellent for both hunting and demonstration flying, but unfortunately they are not common in Britain, being native to the USA and South America. Although they are good birds for many beginners, they cost about £700, which makes them too expensive for all but the most dedicated. They will fly to strange people in strange places as long as there is food about, because they are much more interested in food than in anything that may be going on around them. When hunting, they fly hard and fast, but a trained bird will never go too far from the falconer and the promise of more food. One day, when I can afford it, I'd love to have two Harris's hawks – one for hunting and one for demonstration.

One of the most exciting things you can do with Harris's hawks is what's called 'flying a cast'. That means flying two or more after the same rabbit. In the wild, Harrises work together, with perhaps two on the ground bolting rabbits out of their holes ready for those in the sky to pounce on them. Merlins will also hunt together, three or four of them chasing the same group of skylarks. Most other birds of prey will fight if there's more than one chasing the same prey.

'We'll walk up to that hill top,' said Brian, pointing to some fields beyond his land. 'Take it slowly.'

Along the way Brian talked to us the whole time, not in a loud voice or a whisper, but in a low confident tone, the kind every good falconer adopts when he's in the presence of birds of prey. He was just pointing out little do's and don't's that might not have occurred to the eager amateur. He demonstrated, for example, how to navigate your way over an obstacle like a gate, without disturbing the bird. This is a tricky exercise, but easier if you keep your glove at arm level, shield the bird from the wind with your body, and don't try to jump down the last foot or two, and so jar the bird.

What we were doing was a half-hour walkabout to accustom us to the feel of the birds. We didn't even attempt to fly them, although they were 'bating' in the wind. Brian and I just discussed different techniques and what have you. He knew that I had some experience, but I think he was trying to make me relax and, perhaps, find out just how much I did or didn't know. Then we returned to the house.

We all sat down together again and chatted in general about falconry, and in particular about equipment and how to put it on correctly; how to hold the bird properly; different methods of training a bird; the various illnesses and complaints they suffer from and how to cure them; and simply how to take good care of birds. I noticed that over the four days Brian expanded on these subjects.

Day One we talked a lot about equipment and its use; on the second day about how to handle the birds, and on Day Three Brian went into more detail about care and treatment. Day Four ... well, that was something else – I'll tell you later. Obviously I was learning new things all the time and each day we built on what we had learned the day before. It was fascinating. The equivalent, I suppose, of someone who loves chocolate falling into a big vat of the stuff and unhurriedly eating their way out! I was in my element, immersing myself in all the terms falconers use and studying Brian's vast collection of equipment, some of it quite old and valuable, but in immaculate condition, like his birds.

Apart from the Harris's hawks, we didn't get a chance to pick up any more birds until late on the second day. We were too busy threading jesses and trying out the equipment. Of course, I already had some experience with the various falconers' knots and changing jesses with a bird perched on my fist, but poor old Derek got himself a bit tied up. He patched through it somehow, though.

We must have covered just about everything over those four days, from carrying boxes and travelling with birds to ferreting to keep them fed. Brian was always keen to stress that the comfort and well-being of the birds was of the utmost importance. The bird must always come first, he would tell us over and over again.

'What time's lunch?' Derek would ask, looking at his watch and lighting another cigarette. 'I'm thirsty.'

Naturally, the best bit from my point of view was actually carrying the birds and working with them. On the afternoon of the second day, we put one of the Harris's hawks on a creance, as we would have if we had been training it, and tried a spot of flying. The poor creature must have wondered what was going on, as it was already fully airworthy! We had to fix the unfortunate bird to the creance, place it on its perch in a field, pay out the long line, walk to the place where we wanted it to fly to and hold our gloved hands out with a piece of meat. As we strolled away, however, we had to hold our hands out at arm's length, as if we were under arrest, to show the hawk that we weren't holding a juicy lump of rabbit. Otherwise he'd have been down the line after us like a shot.

Once we were the desired distance away we had to stand perfectly still, reach slowly into our pockets for the food, turn side-on to the bird, look back at it over our shoulders and wiggle the meat. Brian's hawks came for it straightaway. No problem. But Derek and I both made mistakes at first; simple things really, such as accidentally standing on the creance just as the bird came across, so that the poor thing got dumped. But these birds were, as I said, fully trained and could recover from such humiliating blunders by their inexperienced handlers. If you were trying to train one from scratch and made an error like that it could easily mess up an entire day's work.

After each flight we were picked up on little points, such as our positioning or the way we were holding the glove: too high or too low, the wrong angle. One big mistake I made, being used to handling Dawn, was trying to walk the hawk all the way back to its perch. With trained hawks like these, that's like a mother trying to put her teenaged son in a shopping trolley at the local supermarket! They were perfectly capable of going back to the perch without my help. Normally, with Dawn, I would just walk straight towards the perch, but these Harris's hawks were really eager, and bated immediately the breeze got in their feathers; that is, they tried to take off and fly back on their own. They couldn't be allowed to do this, because they were still attached to the creance and might get themselves caught up round the perch.

The solution must have looked quite funny to an onlooker. Picture Derek, or me, walking backwards across a field towards a perch, hawk on glove, trying desperately with our bodies to block the sight of the perch from the alert hawk's vision. The hawk's head would be bobbing and swivelling, trying to find out what on earth was going on. Not until we were a few yards away from the perch could we turn, hold our arms out and release the jesses so that the bird could fly the rest of the way. We soon got the hang of this, though it felt like we were performing a weird new dance. The main thing was that we were picking up a lot of hawking know-how, even if we did look ridiculous.

One of the most enjoyable aspects of the course was the lunch we had in the local pub, which did a particularly memorable steak and kidney pie. (Derek heartily spoke up for the bitter they pulled, too.) I had the pie two days on the trot, it was mouthwateringly tasty. I would have had another one on the third day as well, but I gave it up for the opportunity to go rabbiting with the lad who worked for Brian. Hungry hawks have to be fed, and so a constant supply of fresh meat must be found. The answer is to trap rabbits with ferrets.

I had never done this before and was curious to find out exactly how it was done. So I left Derek and Brian by the door of the pub and headed for the open country.

I was gone for about three hours: scrambling through hedges; rummaging in undergrowth; wrestling with tangled nets; and throwing into a box the indignant ferrets, who after all had done all the work and only wanted to wring the rabbits' necks. For anyone who has never gone 'a-rabbiting', I must say I thoroughly enjoyed it. Basically, you find a warren, cover a few holes with netting, send your ferrets down and wait. This was exciting enough, but little did I know that afternoon how much more exciting hunting rabbits with a hawk could be. I was soon to find out.

The days of our falconry course had a set pattern. First we would sit down and plan out our day; second, we'd decide what we expected to get out of each day, in terms of knowledge and experience; third, we'd go to work, and, finally, we'd meet back at the house in the late afternoon. These end-of-day meetings were very important, for it was then that we reviewed our progress, comparing our morning's expectations with the fruits of our labours. Had we done this? Could we say that we had handled that well? What didn't we do? What had we gained? In this thorough, methodical way we missed out very little indeed.

A fascinating new thing I learned during these sessions was 'feather care', which, of course, comes under the general heading of the bird's health and safety. It's amazing what you learn. I would never have dreamed of doing what Brian demonstrated to us with broken or damaged feathers. You can actually repair or replace feathers, at least primary and secondary ones (the larger wing and tail feathers), by some very ingenious methods. I knew about splicing a broken feather back together, but I didn't know about renovating bent ones.

To splice a feather back together, after a bird has flown into a barbed wire fence, say, or been in a fight, you have to cut off the damaged feather about $\frac{1}{4}$ to $\frac{1}{2}$ inch from the base, take a similar feather from a dead bird and cut it to fit. The quick way to do the repair is to break the point off a needle, dab a bit of glue on the now blunt end and work that into the base or stem of the feather, being careful not to pierce the flesh. Then you gently and gradually work the new feather on, positioning it to match the original plumage as best you can. Do not let the bird preen for at least half an hour or it will just pull the feather out.

This arrangement won't last forever because the needle is too smooth and the feather will slip away from it. The more permanent solution is to use a piece of cane or a cocktail stick instead – this should last until the feather moults naturally.

Obviously it's nice if you can match the colour of the feathers, but a friend of mine had a peregrine that was caught in a bush during a storm, and the only feathers available to effect the repair came from a jackdaw. As almost an entire wing had to be replaced, the peregrine ended up black along one side. This confused bird-watchers, but the bird itself was fine.

I've never had to perform this operation. Dawn has never bent or broken a feather in two and a half years. Kestrels are very prone to tail damage – they have quite a long tail for the size of the bird and in training a leash rubbing against it can snap feathers. When a kestrel I was looking after died recently, I put it in the freezer so that I can use it for 'spares' if necessary.

I loved the way Brian repaired a bent feather. Say a bird has gone after a rabbit and landed awkwardly and got one of its deck feathers (a pair of prominent feathers found in the tail) buckled. How do you straighten it out again? You get a bowl of boiling water and, holding the bird firmly, plunge the bent feather under, making sure, of course, that the scalding water doesn't touch the bird's skin. This makes the hollow stem go rubbery for a few seconds, but then it just stiffens up straight as it cools.

Another interesting technique we learned was how to attach the tail-bell on a kestrel or a falcon. What you do is join the bell to the two middle, or deck, feathers with a strip of leather, threaded with a bell. (Hawks wear bells for the same reason as mountain cattle – so you can hear them when you can't see them.) If you do this awkwardly the bird will obviously be unable to flex open its tail – they don't much anyway, because the deck feathers are the support feathers, like the middle fingers of a human hand. The rest of the tail feathers are more manoeuvrable. But if you restrict the movement too firmly the bird will feel uncomfortable.

How should you place a hood on a bird? What are the different lures for? All these questions were dealt with fully during the course, so Derek and I felt that we had learnt a great deal of new and

ABOVE Inside the local quarry – the owls probably like the peace and quiet, and the leaf litter is full of mice and insects.
BELOW The floor of the quarry is littered with pellets and feathers.

ABOVE The hay barn on a friend's farm. Barn owls used to breed in the hay bales but when these were shifted the birds objected and moved off to the nearby quarry. My friend wanted to encourage them to come back, so we put the bales back where they had been and cut a suitable owl-sized hole in the wall. The owls are often seen outside the barn first thing in the morning, and they nip into the hay when disturbed. We hope they'll breed in the barn again this year.

RIGHT Barn owl eggs in a typical nest. The number of chicks in a clutch varies according to the availability of food and the danger of predators. From any clutch it's possible that one or two wouldn't hatch, and if food was short a little chick might be killed by an elder sibling (or by its mother so that the stronger chick would survive). Two or three chicks surviving is about average for wild birds.

When releasing barn owls
that have been in captivity
for a long time, we keep
them confined to the barn
until we're sure that they
are going to adapt happily
to their new surroundings.
(Hans Reinhard/Bruce
Coleman Ltd)

LEFT A portrait of Zara, my kestrel. Kestrels are popular with audiences at lectures, because they're elegant little birds and also because, of all the British birds of prey, they're the ones people are most likely to spot in the wild: they hover over motorways and are even seen in towns these days. ABOVE Petite, my little owl. Eight and a half inches tall and bad-tempered with it. She tends to react badly to lots of people – it's a sort of stress that is common in older birds – so I don't take her to lectures any more. I'd like to breed from her when I have a bit more space.

Dawn and me, just as I'm about to fly her. I don't care what anyone says, there's no barn owl in the world like her.

fascinating information that we just couldn't have got out of books. I'm not saying you can't read about these things, but you have to have 'hands on' experience to appreciate the subtleties of falconry properly. The course would have been incomplete if it had only been about these technical matters, fascinating as they are. When I look back on it all, the fourth and last day has to be the most exciting and memorable. We were taken hunting with a Harris's hawk.

We arrived as keen as a couple of puppies out for their first walkies, full of fun and raring to go! Brian had to calm us down. Of course, we knew roughly what was in store for us, but it exceeded what we'd imagined. The last day had been set aside for a hunting trip, a full day out in the field, putting into practice, hopefully, all we had learned. We got there a quarter of an hour early, around nine in the morning. The sky was clear and blue with not a cloud even in the west. Perfect weather. Within the hour we'd prepared all the equipment and stored the Harris's hawk in the back of the Land Rover, and we were on our way. (We also took a goshawk in case the Harris's didn't work, but didn't have to fly him.) We'd decided to drive up high on to Bodmin Moor, to a remote farm Brian knew. Derek rode up front with Brian, and I (where else?) cheerfully climbed in the back with the birds.

When we reached the farm the track ran out, so we had a word with the farmer, a friend of Brian's, and set off over the open fields. We'd already spotted several rabbits scampering about. The hawks, hooded and boxed up, brooding, sensing where they were being taken and why, were getting agitated, clicking their tongues and fidgeting. The sense of anticipation was almost unbearable. When Brian braked I was first out of the Land Rover. The Harris's hawk was brought out and took up his position on his master's fist, coldly surveying the land. Nothing stirred. Derek stumbled off into the nearest clump of vegetation and disturbed three petrified rabbits. He got the fright of his life, for the Harris's was at them like a bullet, and he was in the way! The rabbits got clean away.

As we proceeded we kept our eyes skinned and whenever we came to a thicket or undergrowth we beat it with our sticks to stir up the prey. Meanwhile, the magnificent Harris's looked on menacingly. Well, we didn't have much luck out in the open because the rabbits saw or heard or smelt us coming a mile off and bolted down the nearest hole, even though we were mute and trying to stay down

Bald eagle

wind (the wind kept switching direction in little gusts). But we had a few other cards up our sleeves we were waiting to play: we'd brought two furry friends along with us. We were just looking for a suitable warren to send our ferrets down to flush out the occupants.

We didn't have to look far before we found a hollow in the corner of a field, riddled with holes and scattered with fresh earth and droppings. We ended up spending half the day around the area, putting our ferrets down holes and bolting rabbits. In all we had twelve chases. A rabbit would surface and immediately make a bolt for the closest hole when he sensed the hawk. Though not, of course, the one he'd just come up because the ferret was still down there in hot pursuit. Then the hawk would flash down on him. The whole sequence was over in seconds, but it was breathtaking. You would think that these rabbits would have no chance against the combined land and air assaults of ferrets and hawk, but they were incredibly fast and usually disappeared down a safe hole before our Harris's could get hold of them, even though the Harris's hawk moves like lightning.

What really amazed me was the way the hawk seemed to know out of which hole the rabbit was going to pop even before its ears appeared. It was as if the hawk could hear the rabbit running along the tunnels inside the hedge, while he was sitting on a post on top of the hedge. The Harris's expressionless eyes would follow the invisible prey and then fix on its exit. It was uncanny and more than a little unnerving to watch: the perfect hunter at work. Whether he could actually do this or not I don't know. I only know that it was remarkable that he could react so swiftly and swoop down round the rabbit's ears.

Anyway, we didn't have much luck in the hollow either, so we moved further up the field. Now Derek and I were on one side of the hedge, stuffing the ferrets down, and Brian was positioned on the other, with the bird, waiting for the evicted rabbits. I remember one near thing when one scrambled out and ran for some sixty feet along the hedge, pursued instantly by the low-flying hawk. He managed to elude our bird because he was running inside a wire retaining fence and so couldn't be grabbed by the deadly talons. That was one lucky rabbit. It was really frustrating for the hawk – cries of anguish spat from his tongue.

A while later we were across the other side of the hill, trying another hedge. Same plan, only this time we all retreated back some thirty feet so that the wily rabbits wouldn't pick up our scent, to give the bird a chance. Bingo! Our first successful chase. The Harris's gripped like a vice and screeched with delight.

Well, by the end of the day this proved to be our only catch, but we were all three pleased with the day's work. Personally I couldn't have cared less if we hadn't caught a single rabbit. It was worth all the effort just to see the bird do its stuff, and enjoy the indescribable thrill of so many chases. Hunting rabbits with hawks is surely better than blowing their brains out with shotguns. After all, the hawks do actually eat what they catch and you can see how hard the hawk has to work just to get one square meal. It's animal against animal, one on one, which is how it should be. But hawking is labour-intensive and time-consuming and hardly a satisfactory way of keeping rabbit populations down. Rabbits breed like rabbits, you know.

Oh, yes, I never did get a chance to fly that big buzzard. I wonder if he would have had any joy that day . . . only if you tied the rabbits' legs together, I expect.

8

Return to the Wild

I first became involved with releasing barn owls into the wild about two years ago, shortly after I got my first breeding pair, Barny and Mrs Barny. The plight of barn owls, the destruction of their habitat and declining numbers were starting to get more and more media coverage. They were rapidly becoming an endangered species.

Nobody really knows how many barn owls there are left in this country, but various factors have contributed to their decline. The most obvious is that habitats are being destroyed. Barn owls need barns or similar buildings for breeding, and more and more of them are being converted into country houses. An awful lot has been written about the destruction of the hedgerows, but it really does damage the ecology. Barn owls' favourite prey are short-tailed voles, which live in hedgerows along the sides of roads. As hedgerows become rarer, voles have fewer places to live, and as more roads are built crisscrossing the countryside, they stand more risk of being killed by passing cars. Cornwall is luckier than most parts of England in this respect – it's been left alone more than other counties, and lots of applications for planning permission have been turned down. So it's still a pretty good wildlife area – and we must try to keep it that way.

Pesticides have had a damaging effect on a lot of wildlife, including birds of prey, but for some reason this doesn't seem to have affected barn owls as much as the sparrowhawk and peregrine populations. Barn owls are susceptible to bad weather, though, because a hard winter can kill their food supply even if they resist the cold themselves. The last very hard winter we had, in 1978–79, was followed by a noticeable dearth of barn owls.

As I became aware of this, I wondered what could be done to prevent barn owl numbers declining still further. What could I do? I love these birds. I must do something, I thought, so I rang up a friend of mine called David Woolcock. He works at Paradise Park, the sort of bird zoo near Penzance I mentioned earlier. I had some faint ideas about releasing, but David was able to give me some valuable advice on how to go about it.

The first pair we actually released were not ones we had reared. They came into my hands in a rather distressing, but all too familiar, way. A friend of ours, John Pennington, had a farm and campsite near the coast and owned a barn. A mile or so away, there was another barn, a bit more dilapidated, but barn owls don't mind that. They like barns because they provide lots of cover and camouflage – they aren't as resilient as tawny owls, and need more protection from the elements. Ideally, the building should be isolated, so that they can breed in peace. There had been a pair using this barn, but, as so often happens these days, they deserted their nest. The barn was on a main road, and it seems likely that one of the adults was killed and the other went off in search of another mate. This is not unusual, particularly if it's the female who's killed, as the male wouldn't feed the young – that's always the mother's job.

So Derek and I were called in. When we got there we found dead or starving owlets all over the place. It was heart-breaking. We managed to save three with Maureen Edwards's help and between us we nursed them back to health. From these three I took a pair who seemed to get along, for my first release. What better place to release them than their own territory? There was no advantage in taking them back to the barn where they'd been born, as when we found them they were too young ever to have been out of it, so wouldn't have known their way around. But their parents had obviously thought it was a suitable area. As the original barn was quite difficult to get to, I asked John Pennington if I could use his. He was delighted.

Derek and I drove down there and shut off the whole barn, preventing all means of getting in or out. Then we put a box on one of the high window-sills. It was just an ordinary two-floor barn with a ladder from the ground up to the hay loft. The only other way in or out of this upper level was a door for loading bales and what have you. Anyway, we nailed our box to the wall and propped up the front with a piece of wood, to make it stable enough to support the weight of our two owls. Then we wired it over. We positioned it so that it faced away from the doorway, to avoid draughts and to give the future inhabitants a little privacy. Next we searched the entire barn for anything sharp – nails sticking out of the walls, for example – that might cut or harm them. You might think we were being a bit over-cautious, but these were two very young and inexperienced owls we were releasing. They could get quite boisterous and reckless, especially during the early days, when they would be shut in for a while.

When we were satisfied that all the holes in the walls, main door, loft door and roof were sealed up, and nothing could get in or out, we turned our attention to the exterior. First we checked what the food supplies were like in the area simply by looking at what the local cats were bringing in. The farmer and his neighbours were all friends so it was just a case of asking them to keep an eye on their moggies, and spying on a few of the plumper-looking ones – successful hunters, we assumed. There turned out to be plenty of field mice and short-tailed shrews, various larger insects and the odd rat about, so we concluded that there was more than enough food in the vicinity to sustain our pair.

After we'd satisfied ourselves that there was sufficient prey I went off to walk the terrain. It turned out there were a few acres of good hunting land just to the south of the barn. There was also a fairly large stream nearby. And that wasn't all. The fields round the campsite were nice and open and had very good verges, where, of course, most of the owls' prey would be living. Often the verges had been left to grow wild and bushy. It was a perfect example of what the destruction of our hedgerows would mean to all wildlife – they are the very arteries of nature. Just to the north of the barn, some sixty yards or so away, were the cliffs and the land thereabouts was overgrown with ferns. Perfect habitat for our barn owls' prey to feed and reproduce in.

The only road was a quarter of a mile away up a track, leading down to the campsite itself, so that made the immediate area pretty safe. The last thing I wanted was for some motorist to hit one of my owls just when it was establishing itself. A mile along this road was Rocky Valley, which is also a good hunting ground for birds of prey – not necessarily for barn owls, with all the buzzards and kestrels competing, but no doubt our pair would venture over there at some time to see what they could pick up.

So everything seemed okay: the barn was secure, the food supply was better than good and the terrain near perfect. The next stage, of course, was to bring the birds in. As you can see, it isn't just a case of opening a wicker basket and saying 'shoo', like releasing racing pigeons: you have to find the owls a home.

You may be wondering why we wired over the box we installed in the barn. Well, when you release you have to do it in stages, so when we introduced the owls to their new home from the aviary we limited their freedom to the box itself at first. Then we asked John Pennington to drop their food in through the wire, mornings and evenings. In this way we acclimatised them to the sights, sounds and smells around them in the barn.

At the end of a week of this captivity Derek and I dropped by to check on their welfare. They seemed to be doing fine, but just to be on the safe side we gave them another four days to adapt. Then we removed the wire from the front of the box and started feeding them on the ledge. They were now confined to the inside of the barn. We had to be careful when we called round to feed them, though, in case they flew out when we opened the door. It still wasn't time to let them come and go as they pleased. Actually we weren't too happy with the back of the old barn, because although we'd tried to plug up every hole in the stonework, it was still possible for a determined young owl to squeeze out here and there. Therefore we screened off the whole rear of the loft with wire and blankets, and anything else we could lay our hands on. It was either this or rebuild the barn, and our budget didn't run to barn renovation – even for our precious owls!

The occupants of this very undesirable residence with no mod. cons. were gobbling their way through two chicks a day each, which we continued to feed to them on the ledge, right near their box, every morning and late afternoon. Now and then we would feed them twice this number of mice, just to vary their diet. This was tedious work, involving, as you can imagine, a great deal of toing and froing on our part. But it would all be worth it to see them settled and thriving in their new home. I must say Mr Pennington was very co-operative. He went in and fed them for us sometimes, to give us a break, and would phone us up if he thought there were any difficulties. We were going down there every day if possible, or every other day at least. This went on for well over a month, with the owls flying free in the barn, until we were sure they were confident and happy in their surroundings.

When they first started coming out of the box they would just sit wherever they happened to land after stretching their wings. But as time went on they began returning to the box, which was what we wanted them to do. Now we knew they had accepted the box as their home and would probably come back to it even if they were allowed out in the open. So we dismantled the screen over the window and let them fly around the back of the barn. Next we opened up the loading door. They could now come and go whenever they liked. We kept putting food on the ledge for them and they would go out for relatively short flights and then return. But after two weeks of going back and fro to the barn they finally decided for some unknown reason that they had had enough. They just took off and left for good.

It happened one night when Derek and I were down there. We were standing in the loft, watching them flying over the fields for half an hour, until darkness fell and we lost sight of them in the gloom. The next morning there was no sign of them. It was their first major flight away from the barn, and of course we didn't know then it was to be their last. We half expected them to come back a few days later, but they have never returned to the barn we prepared so painstakingly for them, although they are still sometimes seen in the vicinity. They are, however, living close by and were last spotted further up the valley, where they have taken residence in another barn! Well, that's barn owls for you. Obviously Mr Pennington's barn didn't suit – perhaps they objected to the campers.

It doesn't matter – they're in the wild and breeding successfully, I'm pleased to say, and that's all that matters. Even as recently as this summer, for old time's sake, perhaps, one of them was seen hanging round the campsite. The area was clearly suitable, so at least we got something right.

Around this time I had three young ready for release from my original pair, Barny and Mrs Barny. I took them down to Paradise Park for sexing. It's not easy to distinguish the sex of a young bird. You have to take them to an expert to be sure. Well, two of these Barny offspring – they were lucky to be alive, for Mr and Mrs Barny were just about the most brutal parents any owl could be unfortunate enough to have – were paired with Paradise Park birds and remained behind. But the third was also paired up and came home with me. Now I had a pair who were not from the same parents and who seemed fairly suited. At least they weren't tearing each other's feathers out. (I was keen to strain some of the vicious Barny's blood out of any future little owlets, so that they wouldn't grow up to take after their grandfather!) Anyway, I kept them in the aviary for about four weeks just to make sure they would adapt to one another. Then it was time to put them out. By now I had a long list of prospective release sites and sound experience behind me, so things went pretty much according to plan. I find out about these release sites in various ways: through friends or volunteers or the farming parents of children I had lectured to, who have expressed an interest in having a pair and have suitable land. And the list is growing. So I was able to release these two successfully, and had the satisfaction of knowing that they approved of the site I'd chosen.

I get my owls in various ways, too. Many releasings are really re-releasings, that is owls from broken homes, like the first pair, or injured owls I've nursed back to health and paired up. That first year there seemed to be a lot of these about.

In the summer we received a phone call from a lady living up on Davidstow, which is a level stretch of moorland below Roughtor and Brown Willy, the high points of Bodmin Moor. She was worried about a pair of wild barn owls: they had been nesting in her barn for years and she knew there were young up there, but hadn't seen the parent birds going in and out for several days. So Derek and I went to investigate. We drove out straight away with a bagful of food. As soon as we arrived we were shown a dead chick. What would we find in the loft?

The only way we could get up to the nest was to borrow a ladder from a neighbouring farmer and climb up. With heavy heart, fearing the worst, I felt round in the cold nest. Nothing. The barn floor below was covered in strands of hay and there was an old baler parked in the middle. After an hour of feeling around on our hands and knees, sadly, we found another dead chick. Next we looked outside in the field where the barn owner had discovered the other dead owlet, and found two more, both dead. By now we had been there several hours and things weren't looking very optimistic. There didn't seem much point in searching for more corpses. We were ready to leave but the lady insisted that we keep looking, she was convinced there were more. Then Derek had a bright idea: why not look inside the baler?

It was an old thing with spikes and flaps which you could lift up and down to get at the mechanics. Derek lifted up one of these squeaky casings and there, sitting in a row on an oily shaft, were three baby barn owls. They were close to starvation and – typical of barn owls when they're frightened – they sat as stiff as dummies, not making a sound. They must have fallen from the loft and hopped inside, and touched something in there that brought the rusty flap crashing down to entomb them. Another day and they'd have been as dead as doornails.

I wriggled down underneath the contraption and found a fourth, barely alive. This one eventually died, but I'm delighted to say that, with Maureen's assistance, the other three all survived. Maureen showed me how to insert food down their throats to force-feed them, because when birds are in shock like this they just won't eat. In the end we released two of these three lucky ones back to the same barn they were born in. We'll never know why their parents deserted them (maybe pesticides got them), but I'm sure their offspring won't lose any sleep over it. These things happen in the animal world. A human family would never return to such a scene of grisly death, but the owls just took it all calmly.

This re-releasing is unfortunately often necessary because man breaks the delicate balance owls have with their habitat. As the habitat shrinks, parents abandon their young to lessen the competition for food. More often than not when I'm called out it's to find an owl has been poisoned, trapped or shot. Obviously, when parents are killed a whole generation is wiped out at a stroke. Need I say more?

Poisoning and how to deal with it is one of the skills you have to learn when you're dealing with sick birds. The tell-tale signs of poisoning in birds are lethargy, refusing to feed and discoloration of the eyes. The remedy is quite messy, at least one of the remedies. It entails beating up some chicken eggs, putting them into a syringe and squirting the uncooked scramble down the bird's throat. This makes it vomit and gives it diarrhoea, so you're flushing the toxins out of both ends. Sometimes you've got to be a little cruel to be kind!

One of the most lovable, if not *the* most lovable (apart from Dawn), owlets I have ever had the pleasure to meet was Biggles. Biggles – we named him that because of his flying, or should I say crashing, antics – had the misfortune to be one of Barny's babies. He was knocked around so much by his father that he ended up with a crooked leg, but he must have had some courage, because he was the only one of his clutch to survive. He was, however, failing to thrive, so Maureen and I decided to take him away from Barny and put him into care, so to speak. Maureen nursed him back to reasonable health in her bedroom. Every day after school I would rush round to her house to see how he was getting on and take a turn at feeding him.

Once he was on the mend, we decided to try and do something about his crooked leg. Maureen came up with the ingenious idea of making a sling. It looked just like a sailor's hammock made out of toilet paper, cotton wool and string. The idea was to put him in it from time to time to give his gammy leg a rest. Unfortunately, it didn't seem to do much good, but it was to come in very useful later. Another problem was his feathers: he wasn't growing down quickly enough and he was always shivering, so Maureen made him a little coat out of cotton wool. He did look strange, wearing his woolly jacket and swinging in his sling! The coat helped. A month later his down had grown through and he wasn't shaking so much. If I tell you that Maureen actually had to give him the kiss of life twice when he caught a chill, you'll appreciate why we went to such lengths to keep him warm.

Anyway, by the time Maureen went on her annual holiday, Biggles was feeding himself a bit and coming on well, so I took over. I even learnt how to change his soiled coat. I kept him in Maureen's bedroom, despite Mum's protests. All the time Maureen was away she was worrying herself sick about Biggles. She even sent him a postcard. She was really pleased when she came back and found him fighting fit, even though he was still using one wing as a crutch to support his crooked leg. We decided it was time to do something about that, so we took him along to the vet.

The vet said there wasn't much he could do because he didn't think Biggles was old enough or strong enough to survive the anaesthetic. We said he was stronger than he looked, but the vet turned us away and told us to bring him back when he was bigger. We tried to pull the leg up so that he wouldn't put so much weight on it, but then he only found it even harder to walk straight. His stumbling gait took him off in all directions except the one he wanted to go in. If he wanted to reach an object he had to set out in the wrong direction and hope to angle in on it! He actually found it easier to walk backwards. He even flew backwards sometimes, though how he managed this I'll never know.

Three weeks went by and we were back at the vet's surgery. This time the vet cut a V out of Biggles's crippled leg bone and thought that might do the trick. We put him back in the sling-hammock to give him a chance to heal. After five days we removed the packing around the splint. It was looking good. Two days later we took off the splint. Now the wing only dropped slightly. It was a definite improvement. Biggles seemed to think so, too.

By now he had become imprinted on Maureen. That means he thought Maureen was his mother, so I gave him to her. He's still just as comical and lives with Maureen to this day. I don't know why, but he seems to detest me – every time I go round to see him he hisses at me. Well, he is Barny's son, after all!

Not all stories have happy endings, however. Before raising Biggles we had a few failures with baby owls the shocking Barnys had abused. But caring for Biggles taught us a lot. I tried rearing owlets in my bedroom under heat lamps several times, usually without much success. Come to think of it, I always seem to have baby owls in my bedroom. Perhaps that's why it smells so terrible in there.

One particular owl that sticks in my mind was one I kept alive for six weeks, in the early days. He seemed to be doing fine and then one night I found him cold and dying. I cuddled him for four hours until he died in my hands. I was very upset, even though I had seen a lot of birds die before; I had really thought this one was going to make it. I'm afraid this is just something you have to get used to, like a nurse in a hospital – it goes with the job. Still, more make it these days, I'm glad to say. I hope to rear another barn owl like Dawn some day, from the egg to the jesses. That would really be something.

9

The Prince's Trust Award

B reeding owls and travelling around the West Country giving lectures on them in schools and the like can be an expensive pastime. I've never charged a fee for anything I've done and so all my work has had to be financed out of my own pocket. I'm not grumbling, after all it is my hobby. But for a schoolboy, you will appreciate this was not easy, and became more and more difficult as the amount of lecture work and breeding costs increased. Although in the early days Derek was happy to drive me around and didn't even charge me for the petrol, pretty soon our visits here and there grew so frequent and far afield that he was finding himself quite a bit out of pocket. Generally, anyone who invited me to lecture did pay travelling expenses without my having to ask, but there were a lot of other people and places – like farmers and release sites – we had to visit, not to mention collecting food and injured birds. Fuel costs were really starting to mount up, so I felt I had to contribute something.

By the autumn of 1989 I could see that the work I was planning, more breeding and lecturing, was going to get very costly. My long-suffering owl chauffeur said to me one day while he was yet again driving me to some venue I was going to give a talk at, 'You and that bird are costing me a bloody fortune!'

I knew Derek really enjoyed our trips and was only kidding, but I was thinking of ways in which I could raise more money to pay my share. I was already working as Derek's apprentice carpet-fitter in my spare time – when I had any – but the wage I was getting was going not only on the birds' upkeep but also on mine. I had to give Mum something. It was getting to the point where it was either me or the birds!

About this time a new librarian, Suzy Chaplin, arrived at our school and she took a keen interest in anything the students were doing. I was chatting to her one lunch-time and just happened to mention that I kept and bred barn owls. She showed immediate enthusiasm and, well, one thing led to another and before long I had invited her and her family to come over to Tintagel to meet Dawn and see her fly. This was to prove a very fortunate meeting.

The following week Suzy, her husband and daughter, turned up and were really thrilled to see the birds, especially Dawn, who captured all their hearts. Later on that week we were talking in the library again and somehow the topic of owls came up in conversation once more. I must have mentioned how expensive my activities were becoming, because Suzy suggested that I tried applying for a grant.

This was news to me. I didn't think you could get grants for your hobby; I thought they were for businesses and things like that. But Suzy said there were all kinds of awards young people could get, particularly if what they were doing was connected with conservation – I was really surprised. She also said she would find out more information about a few of them for me. Within two days she had found some information on the Prince's Trust, which is a scheme set up by the Duke of Cornwall, HRH Prince Charles himself. I laughed. The thought of asking one of the Royal Family for money to breed owls seemed a bit out of order; however, Suzy explained that the scheme was designed to help young people just like myself set up projects or businesses which are of benefit to the local community, as well as themselves. I was still doubtful, but Suzy said she thought the work I was doing fitted this description perfectly and encouraged me to apply.

I felt a little embarrassed about putting myself forward, but she nagged me until I wrote a letter and posted it off. Even when my application was on its way I still couldn't convince myself that what I was doing was likely to qualify for any kind of grant. I put it out of my mind.

A week or so went by and I hadn't received a reply. Then suddenly I had a phone call, which really was out of the blue because if anything I had been expecting a letter. A man who represented the regional office of the Prince's Trust in Truro was ringing to ask for more information about my work. He asked me about costs and what exactly I'd been doing. I told him everything he wanted to know. He thanked me and said that my application would be on the table for consideration at the next meeting of the committee.

Just over a week into December I received an early Christmas present: a letter from the Prince's Trust containing a cheque for

£200! I had been awarded something I never dreamed I'd be eligible for. The letter said that the work I was doing with barn owls was very worthwhile and deserving, and the Trust wished to publicise it further with my permission. Of course I agreed. I hadn't known that I was going to be presented with such a large sum. It was great. Two days later they phoned up to confirm that the cheque had arrived and congratulated me. Then they discussed what they had in mind for the publicity. My mouth fell open. Basically, they wanted to write a press release about me and distribute it to all the local newspapers, Radio Cornwall, Television South West and the BBC regional news programme, *Spotlight*. I was staggered. The BBC actually interviewed me for *Spotlight*, both at home, flying Dawn, and at Sir James Smith's school, giving a lecture. I'll tell you more about it in the next chapter. I've still got the video of it. It gave me quite a thrill.

This recognition by the Prince's Trust gave me more than just financial help. It was to have a big effect on my whole life. Things started to look up for me. It seemed that everyone wanted to know about what I was doing. If someone had told me a month before that my life was going to be changed so dramatically, I would not have believed them. And it got me thinking that there must be thousands of people up and down the country doing worthwhile things to protect our environment and wildlife who go unrecognised. I felt very lucky. But then when people are driving at night and catch a glimpse of a barn owl in their headlights, they should feel lucky, too.

10

A Little Bit of Fame

I used to be known as Jon Hadwick, but after the award from the Prince's Trust and the follow-up publicity, I started to be called things like the 'Owl Boy' or 'Bird Boy'. People who didn't know me or know where I lived but had heard or read about me were sending me letters that just said 'To the Owl Boy, Owl House, Tintagel' on the envelope. I guess the postman got used to it after a while, although there are two other people in the village who keep owls.

It was incredible what a little bit of publicity could do. I had post coming in from all over the place, from children who wanted to know more about owl-keeping and old age pensioners who just wanted to say how pleased they were that there were still some youngsters who didn't spend their lives roaming the streets and vandalising everything in sight! Although I'm not a vandal, I didn't always feel that the praise I received was justified. I'm no saint (am I, Mum?), but I don't have much opportunity to get up to much teenage mischief, even if I wanted to. Owls are too time-consuming.

Articles about me were appearing everywhere, cropping up like mushrooms on an autumn morning. I was in all the local papers and it wasn't long before the nationals picked up the story too. Then, as I mentioned earlier, BBC *Spotlight* rang up one evening and said they wanted to come to Tintagel to do an item on me. I said I'd be delighted, although I felt a bit nervous. To make me even more anxious they insisted that they film me doing one of my lectures at school. I had to telephone our deputy head, Mr Kitching, who is responsible for community links, to make sure it would be okay. But there was no problem. Mr Kitching was very pleased, and so the next morning it was all arranged.

There was a knock at the door. My heart pounding, I opened it and was confronted by the *Spotlight* film crew: interviewer John Francis, a cameraman and sound recordist.

'Good morning, Jon – now let's have a look at these owls,' said the men from the BBC.

We walked up to Derek's field and I got Dawn out on my fist. It didn't take long for them to take a few shots and we were soon all back in my house, having a cup of tea. Derek came round and we loaded Dawn and the equipment into the car, as we had done so many times before. Then we drove the four miles to school, followed by the film unit in their car.

Mr Kitching met us in reception and escorted us to one of the art rooms which had been chosen as our venue. It is large and, being an art room, full of light. A class of second years were dragged in from down the corridor to be my audience, as this one was strictly for the camera. When I walked in with Dawn they gave us a great reception. Meanwhile, the film crew had set up a 2000-watt lamp in the corner. Dawn took it all in her stride, like the professional that she now was. Next the interviewer and I sorted out a few questions for me to be asked and fed them to the audience – it was all so staged. Anyway, I did my lecture – a shortened version, lasting just ten minutes – answered a few general questions, and then John Francis interviewed me one to one. This part had to be filmed twice as my answers were far too long for television purposes. Once I get going I just can't stop talking. And then they filmed Dawn flying diagonally across the room, over the heads of the excited second years, from Derek to me. It all seemed to go quite well and was shown that evening, although they had obviously cut out quite a bit by then.

It might have been only a short piece of film, but within one and a half minutes of the end of *Spotlight* our phone rang. I was booked to do a lecture at St Kew school. Other callers followed rapidly. Some wanted advice on keeping owls or just rang to tell me they had them living nearby; others wanted to get me to do a lecture for some group or other. It went on like this until about 10.30 at night, and then we just had to stop answering the phone altogether. For the first one and a half hours it worked out at one phone call every five to ten minutes. After this it fell off to about three per hour. I was exhausted, but at the same time fascinated by the power of the media.

Two days later post started pouring in. I received several letters from various owl trusts, asking about my breeding and work in the area, as well as many other people expressing interest in what I was doing. I replied to as many as I could; some didn't actually ask for a reply, but just congratulated me.

As I had already appeared in local papers it was now the turn of the 'big' boys who worked for the nationals. The *Daily Mail, Daily Telegraph* and *Guardian* all did articles on us. Most of their stories followed a similar line: 'A sixteen-year-old schoolboy, Jon Hadwick, of Tintagel . . .' etc, etc, and had titles like, 'Hoots of . . .' something or other, and other predictable plays on owl words. Needless to say I kept all the cuttings.

Soon I got a phone call from the BBC asking for more information about owls. There was mention of a spot on *Wildlife on One, Pebble Mill, Going Live* or *Blue Peter*. Nothing has come of any of this yet, but you never know!

Abbey National's magazine, *Ace*, which is given out to staff and investors, did a one-page colour feature on us, headed 'Owl Boy'. It made me sound like a comic strip hero, I thought, like Batman or Spiderman; perhaps I'd be hopping round to crimes calling, 'Hoot! Hoot! It's the winged crusader!'

In September 1990 *Country Life* were doing an article on the Prince's Trust and phoned me up to ask what I thought of it. I told them I thought the Trust was wonderful, but magazines work several months in advance and when last heard this article hadn't been published yet.

Then I received a call from a company called Acrobat Designs who wanted to use Dawn for the new phone card publicity brochures and posters, part of Telecom's endangered species series: the otter, red squirrel and barn owl, of course, are all in danger of extinction. All three, however, can still be found in Cornwall. They asked me to go up to London, to their offices just off Vincent Square, where they took many photographs of Dawn flying past their illustrators. That was really interesting. To get the right shots – they wanted ones of the underside of Dawn as she was flying – they had to set up an elaborate ploy. We were all in this sort of basement which had a balcony; a cameraman was positioned at the foot of some stairs leading up to the balcony and I was standing, with Dawn, a little way in front of him, with a big screen behind us. As I released her she was meant to fly to Derek, not on to the balcony as she did. Well, it took a few attempts but at last they got the photographs they wanted.

And now I'm writing this book. I suppose when it comes out next spring it'll all start up again. I don't mind; I'm looking forward to it, though I must say that at the time of writing, or rather of finishing the book, it is almost midwinter and I am feeling quite exhausted. One way and another it has been a pretty hectic year for me. As I actually write these last few thoughts down it is one o'clock in the morning and I have just returned from a weekend in London. I have been staying with friends in a youth hostel on a school trip, and taking the opportunity to have a look round a few galleries and art exhibitions. I'm in the sixth form now at Sir James Smith's school, taking A level art. Obviously, there are already a few bird paintings in my portfolio of work for the examiners, but I've also been encouraged to start doing some life drawing and landscapes. And I'm quite pleased with the results.

It's one of my ambitions to be a successful artist. I've already had some success in this direction. Several of my line drawings of birds sold earlier this year for what I considered a large sum of money, even before they reached the London gallery they were on their way to! So I feel encouraged to do more. In fact I have over thirty more drawings and a few water-colours at home, finished and framed, but I'm striving to improve and broaden my canvas, so to speak. Recently I've tried working in acrylics, a new medium for me, and I like the brightness of colours I can achieve (great for plumage!) and texture. They also dry quicker. Anyway, I've been looking at the sort of things that are selling in London in and around the galleries; checking out the market and studying the different techniques. With my family's help, both in terms of encouragement and finance, particularly from my nan and uncle, I hope to extend this side of my work in the future. I want to earn enough money to put myself on my feet. So I'm looking to raise my standard to a professional level, introduce more variety of subject (though always specialising in birds), have a few exhibitions and generally find more ways of distributing and selling my work.

Apart from my art, I want to keep up my lecturing on birds around the South West, and maybe farther afield. But I especially want to acquire a few more display birds. I'd love to have a European eagle owl. It's a very big and spectacular bird and would be excellent for displays and lectures. It's one of the largest of the owls, and as people are always asking how big the biggest owl is, it would have educational value as well as being a lovely bird to train.

I've already talked about the Harris's hawk; the Lanner falcon is another bird I'd love to have. It's an extremely fast flyer and responds very well to the lure – it would be easy to train in the way I'd trained Dawn, and the results would be very impressive. The Lanner is much like a peregrine in flight and has great manoeuvrability as well as speed. It isn't so good for hunting, though, so this would be for display only.

Until recently I had a kestrel, and I hope to get another soon. People always love to see these elegant little birds, particularly as they're the birds of prey most commonly seen in the wild.

Then I'd like to have a variety of owls that may not be much good for flying displays but which look attractive, ones people would like to come and see. I've got a little owl – I call her Petite – that I used to take to lectures, but she's getting a bit stroppy in her old age, so she has to stay at home now. It'd quite common for birds of prey to become aggressive later in life when they're kept in captivity – I guess it's frustration. So I may sell Petite, or use her for breeding. It used to be quite funny when I took her to lectures, because I'd say she was a little owl and people would say, 'Well, yes, we can see that, but what *sort* of little owl?' They didn't understand that that's what the species is called. A little owl is about 8½ inches tall when fully grown, and Petite's 'fed-up' weight is six ounces; her flying weight used to be five ounces.

Neither the long-eared nor the short-eared owl is really large enough to train for hunting, but they're good for educational purposes – they're appealing to look at, particularly the long-eared with its ear tufts (they're only extended feathers and don't affect the hearing at all), and you can use them to show children first hand what an owl is like. They're found in many parts of Britain, though not much in Cornwall, but it does give people something to look out for.

As I've mentioned already, I've acquired a red-tailed buzzard. This is an American bird (it's called a red-tailed hawk over there) but it's better for hunting than our common buzzard – it's slightly faster and bigger, and therefore can handle larger prey. They mainly hunt rabbits, but the fastest of them can catch hares, moorhens, pheasants and squirrels too. I'm flying her more often than Dawn at the moment because I'm building her up as a hunting and display bird. Buzzards have a crop in which they can store food, so the delicate balance of feeding is not quite so crucial, but the food works through their system much faster in cold weather. All birds need to

Little owl

be fed more when the temperature drops.

There are other British birds of prey I'd love to work with in the future: merlins have always appealed to me, though their size makes them vulnerable. A male may weigh as little as four ounces, which means the slightest miscalculation in their ideal flying weight could be fatal; they are also susceptible to accident or predators, and at £300 a time, you don't want to risk losing too many of them. The sparrowhawk is a marvellous hunting bird and a superb acrobat in the air. Its main prey is small birds, which are easier to flush than rabbits, so a sparrowhawk wouldn't be as time-consuming as some other hunting birds – you'd probably only need to hunt with it for an hour or two a day. The hobby isn't a very good hunter, so if I got one of those it would be purely for my own interest. That'll have to wait till I'm more experienced with falcons.

And then – maybe when I retired – I'd want to have a golden eagle. They're renowned for being temperamental and difficult to handle, so it would be best to hunt them up on the moors, certainly well away from any towns or too many people. For anybody who's really keen on falconry, the golden eagle is the ultimate bird of prey, but I suspect this is a long way in the future for me.

I think if I could get a good collection of British birds together, people would be more interested than they would be in a show of purely foreign birds. The reason for this is twofold. First, it's good to show what people could actually expect to see in the wild if they got themselves a decent pair of binoculars and had some patience. And secondly, it brings home the idea of conservation of our own wildlife. People would see how beautiful our native birds of prey are and say, 'Wow! Do all these birds really live in the British Isles? That's wonderful. They must be protected.'

Anyway, that's the general plan. Of course, my big interest is still falconry and so building up from my display collection I want to go further and get together a selection of hunting birds for sport. I'd like a falcon for chasing rooks, crows and jackdaws – birds like that, whose numbers must be controlled if other, rarer birds are to survive. With the demise of so many of our native falcons in some areas, magpie populations have been ballooning over the last couple of decades, so I'd like a falcon capable of hitting magpies. Having the whole range of British hunting birds would be my ideal goal. Plus, of course, a breeding and releasing programme for each.

Merlin

But this would be a tremendous amount of work and I'd need to employ others to help me, and it presupposes there'll still be enough habitat to release birds into.

All this is leading up to my ultimate aim in life: owning and running my very own Falconry and Conservation Centre in North Cornwall, complete with aviaries and staff, which I would need to have if I was to keep all the birds I would like. It would be somewhere I could do displays in the summer for the paying public, and relax in the winter and do some hunting; then get down to some serious painting. I'd have the birds close at hand to help improve my art, which might even bring me in a bit more money to help pay for the upkeep of the centre. So my two hobbies would support each other and everything would be perfect. Well, I can dream.

On the immediate horizon I need a car, which would give a good impression when I go to meetings and lectures. It would have to be an estate or hatchback so that I could transport the birds. And so I'm taking driving lessons, and saving up.

Breeding and releasing is uppermost on my mind at the moment. There is much work to be done and I seem to have been busy doing lots of other things recently. Some day I'd like to link up with Paradise Park and the Barn Owl Trust in Devon, which both run breeding and releasing schemes. I'd like to be a sort of halfway house, midway between the two of them, covering North and East Cornwall, looking after birds of prey in my local area, interbreeding with these other places. Obviously I have to build up my reputation, find a suitable site, raise tons of money . . . it's a tall order, but it's the thing I really want to do in this life.

At present I'm getting together some artwork for a Crafts Fair across the border in Devon this weekend, which I've been invited to join by the organisers. And then, of course, this book will come out and after that I'd like to develop my writing, too; publish a few sequels, perhaps, or even something in a different vein. I've always thought a thriller on the illegal trade in rare birds would make a good book and be topical. So everything's moving along in the right direction for me.

Basically, I want to link up my art, my lectures, my displays, hunting, breeding and releasing, and writing; pull them all together to give me one big job that I'd thoroughly enjoy doing for the rest of my life. My first love will always be birds, so I don't think I could ever do a job that wasn't connected with them. Birds of prey are so demanding to keep that if I had another job, I wouldn't have enough time for them. Time to fly them, feed them and care for them. It just wouldn't be fair on the birds. I'd have to give them up. But that's never going to happen, because I have every intention of fulfilling most of my ambitions. I've already come a long way along the road, and I'm going to keep working at it.

So if you should come down to North Cornwall in, say, ten years from now – the year 2000 – look up Hadwick's Falconry Centre in the Yellow Pages. You never know, I just might be in there. Do come and see me – and the birds, of course!